Selective Forex Trading

Founded in 1807, John Wiley & Sons is the oldest independent publishing company in the United States. With offices in North America, Europe, Australia, and Asia, Wiley is globally committed to developing and marketing print and electronic products and services for our customers' professional and personal knowledge and understanding.

The Wiley Trading series features books by traders who have survived the market's ever changing temperament and have prospered—some by reinventing systems, others by getting back to basics. Whether a novice trader, professional, or somewhere in-between, these books will provide the advice and strategies needed to prosper today and well into the future.

For a list of available titles, please visit our Web site at www.WileyFinance.com.

Selective Forex Trading

How to Achieve Over 100 Trades in a Row Without a Loss

DON SNELLGROVE

BICENTENNIAL
1807
WILEY
2007
BICENTENNIAL

John Wiley & Sons, Inc.

Published by John Wiley & Sons, Inc., Hoboken, New Jersey.
Published simultaneously in Canada.

Wiley Bicentennial Logo: Richard J. Pacifico

For general information on our other products and services or for technical support, please contact our Customer Care Department within the United States at (800) 762-2974, outside the United States at (317) 572-3993 or fax (317) 572-4002.

Wiley also publishes its books in a variety of electronic formats. Some content that appears in print may not be available in electronic formats. For more information about Wiley products, visit our Web site at www.wiley.com.

Library of Congress Cataloging-in-Publication Data:

Snellgrove, Don, 1947–
    Selective Forex trading : how to achieve over 100 trades in a row without a loss / Don Snellgrove.
        p. cm. – (Wiley trading series)
    Includes index.
    ISBN 978-0-470-12083-5 (cloth)
    1. Foreign exchange market.   2. Foreign exchange futures.   3. Speculation.   I. Title.
    HG3851.S62 2008
    332.4′5–dc22

                                                                2007034461

Printed in the United States of America.
10 9 8 7 6 5 4 3 2 1

Contents

Legalities: As of 2007, the foreign currency exchange continues to be an unregulated industry. At the time this book was being written, only forex brokers who voluntarily register with regulators are subject to fines and other overseeing efforts like those found in other markets such as stocks, futures, and commodities. The reason I have posted disclaimers so many times within this book is because the forex may be a dangerous market for traders who do not spend time learning the skill of trading in the forex. The following is a partial general disclaimer that is used by many brokerages.

DISCLAIMER

Trading the foreign exchange market carries a high level of risk and may not be suitable for all investors. Before deciding to trade the foreign exchange market, you should carefully consider your investment objectives, level of experience, and risk appetite. The possibility exists that you could sustain a loss of some or all of your initial investment; therefore, you should not invest money that you cannot afford to lose. You should be aware of all the risk associated with foreign currency exchange trading, and you should seek advice from an independent financial advisor if you have any doubts.

Acknowledgments

Thank you to my wife Barbara for her ongoing support of my career as a trader. Thanks also to CJ Shires and the guys at CFG for their help with the research and illustrations found within this book. A special thank-you is extended to the developer of the SmartCharts, Gerald Greene.

Congratulations to the many traders who have traded 50, 100, and even 200 plus trades in a row without a loss on live trading accounts while using stops to protect their margins. Your success using the S90/Crossover and other proprietary techniques of a CFG trader provided the encouragement that I needed to write this book.

Read This First!

*Are You Ready for Something
Different in the World of Trading?*

W ho should read this book about proprietary trading techniques within the foreign currency exchange, also known as the forex? This book is for beginning, intermediate, and advanced traders who need to increase the odds of successful trades by making precise entries. This means making precise decisions regarding entry selections. This book is for those of you who need to have sustaining income as you develop your personal trading skills. This book is not intended for successful traders who have found a procedure that works, and the information contained within this book is in no way intended to put down other methodologies, traditional trading procedures, or trading styles.

The approach presented in this book is a different type of methodology that uses nontraditional proprietary trading tools and must not be integrated with traditional methodology. Merging traditional tools that use other mathematical calculations, patterns, and procedures into these new concepts may cause losses. Change and modernization of trading tools, or simply change, may offend experienced traders; again, allow me to reiterate that this is not my intention in writing this book. My suggestion is that if you are successful and happy with your present status regarding trading success and profits, then why read this book? "If it isn't broken, then don't fix it," as some would say; however, if you feel you have not arrived as a successful forex trader, then read on—because maybe this book is just what you have been searching for. I simply ask that you keep an open mind and try not to merge the trading tools of the smaller markets with the modernized tools of this very large and volatile market known as the forex.

The methodology explained and illustrated throughout this book is only one of many approaches to trading the forex. The system became known by many traders who attended Concorde Forex Group (CFG) training seminars after the concept of time com-pression comparison and the procedural methodology were first introduced in 2002. The system became famous because the CFG organization was the first to produce forex traders who have traded 50, 100, 200, and even 400+ trades consecutively without a loss.* Traders are constantly trying to beat string records, and I have heard that many have set goals to reach 1,000+ trades in a row without a loss. I have also met traders who have failed at trading while attempting to use the CFG procedures due to misinter-pretation or merging them with other methodologies. And I have met other traders who boasted success but either used no protective stops or used improper backstops (which I refer to as very large gambling backstops) to achieve the successful consecutive trading results.

The good news is that enough traders who were part of a large test group success-fully followed the S90/Crossover© and extreme level (EL) instructions, including the ap-plications, while using proper protection to validate the duplication of the procedural methodology. The success of traders within the study group gave me the encouragement and motivation to share the trading approach and applications with those traders who sincerely want to attempt to increase their odds of having success trading the forex.

Here are seven suggestions and points of advice to consider:

1. Follow the rules of a simple trading approach. Keep it simple.

2. Accept responsibility for personal decisions and actions in the market. No one—and no methodology—is responsible for your interpretation of the market.

3. Make sure you trade a demo or play money (paper trade) successfully before moving into the world of live trading. Once you are ready to trade live, then consider trading on a live mini account, with a very small amount of deposited margin to ease into the world of live trading. It is not only an emotional learning experience to gain control of but sometimes a very stressful event in one's life to move from trading demo money to trading live money. Once you have achieved success with a small live mini account, then you can move on to the larger standard accounts, where risk becomes greater as well as potential profits.

4. Establish a live account with a broker who is known for integrity. Brokers who play games such as holding trades in order for the market to have time to turn in order

---

Disclaimer: Trading the foreign exchange market carries a high level of risk and may not be suit-able for all investors. Before deciding to trade the foreign exchange market, you should carefully consider your investment objectives, level of experience, and risk appetite. The possibility exists that you could sustain a loss of some or all of your initial investment; therefore, you should not invest money that you cannot afford to lose. You should be aware of all the risk associated with foreign currency exchange trading, and you should seek advice from an independent financial ad-visor if you have any doubts.

to capture your money for their gain are not playing a fair game. Reputations follow brokers who hold markets during slow and fast moments of volume.

Note: Always plan a trade that has more than a scalper mentality of gaining only 1 to 5 pips. This way, the broker has ample time to cover a submitted trade or pass it on through to a bank or clearinghouse. Data feeds are different for most brokers, depending on their source, and you should allow a broker a little chance to make money as well. After all, without a broker, the opportunity to trade in the markets would be very expensive. More will be offered on this value and need for brokers within the industry.

5. Invest in personal education before trading the forex, even if you have experience trading other markets. The forex is a totally different type of industry, with much more volatility than other markets. When selecting a firm or mentor to assist you in developing the skills necessary to survive your initial years trading the forex, and as you develop those skills, make sure the mentoring person or company is walking the talk. Many mentors teach but do not trade, and this may not be the best way for you to learn. A legitimate mentoring company or individual not only is trading live but is in a position to provide ongoing free daily support along with a proven track record of success to back up the ability to teach. Good mentors will have on file, for anyone to review, copies of documented live trading histories from students that they or their organizations have trained.

6. The greatest distance to overcome in each trade is found between the ears. I feel attitude is everything in the markets, and that is why I have placed so much emphasis on becoming a string trader. Many have told me that the truth comes out about yourself when you learn how to trade. You may learn much more about your self-discipline as a forex trader than you have ever realized if you keep an open mind as you pay your dues of time and practice. More will be covered in future chapters on why you should strive to be a string trader and how this may straighten out issues regarding lack of discipline in the market.

7. You must persevere in the market, never giving up while learning and paying the dues of time. It is necessary to just hang in there even if it takes years trading a demo and a live mini account before you are ready to move into the world of standard account trading. All too often, traders go live way too soon and lose their money because they skipped the necessary steps of paying the dues of practice, spending time in the market, as well as just growing and finding out who they are. Trading definitely will reveal something about yourself that you may have never known.

Reminders of the preceding statements are included at the beginning of some chapters, to help keep you on track regarding the focus and caution you need in the marketplace.

The S90/Crossover began with a dream at a very stressful time during the beginning of my skill development. I monitored and studied the pattern carefully, then—since there was nothing to be found anywhere on the net or within my attorney's legal search—I filed for a copyright. The name comes from S for Snellgrove, 90 for a minimum of 90 percent success on targets and entry points, and the crossover is because all the support lines will have to cross through the market to either create a future legal or illegal target.

My hope is that this methodology may allow currently unsuccessful forex traders as well as neophyte traders the opportunity to build a consecutive and profitable trading portfolio with a minimum of losses. When a trading failure does occur, the second objective is to exit the trade with a minimal loss to avoid losing profits that were gained during the disciplined approach to successful trading that CFG is constantly promoting to traders around the world.

Also, throughout this book are "million-dollar tips" in boxes, and I recommend you reread each one several times.

Please note these three points about what you'll find in this book:

1. Disclaimers are placed throughout this book to remind all traders and potential beginners of the dangers found within the industry.

2. Basic concepts are reiterated or duplicated a few times to remind traders of the importance of clearly understanding procedures of the S90/Crossover.

3. A few of the charts were taken from the studies of different professional live traders so that you may see the actual chart as viewed by the trader and know what the screen looked like during a trade. Vertical, horizontal, diagonal, and Fibonacci lines are drawn everywhere it seems on some of the illustrations and are there for personal reasons. It's okay to draw on charts, and it is good for you to see how traders really look at charts during their studies; this is the reason for the marked-up charts that are included and referenced in this book.

The following explanation is necessary regarding the trading tools being used as illustrations:

Any charting service that will offer the extreme levels of larger time compressions on a daily basis as well as the River Oscillator Indicator (ROI), G meter, and stochastics while having multiple time compressions will be a satisfactory alternative to the charts used here for illustrative purposes. The illustrations in this book are taken with proper written permission from the Forex Producers Group, LLC and CFGSmartCharts service, which displays the inner channel walls and extreme levels. These levels appear exclusively on CFGSmartCharts as well as the Forex Producers charting service, and the levels automatically update approximately every 24 hours, indicating range shifting in process as well as a possible trend shift. Other charting services may offer the levels; however, the trader must draw the lines personally on the charts daily, which may delay or limit the number of combinations for a day of trading.

CHAPTER 1

Advice and Thoughts for Neophyte, Intermediate, and Advanced Traders

"Accept responsibility for your personal decisions and actions in the market. When it is time for the actual entry into the market, and if you are making the final decision to enter, then no one, and no methodology, is responsible for your interpretation of the market. Here's the bottom line: You are on your own if and when you push the entry button."

I made that statement in front of approximately 800 traders at the 2004 CFG Traders Conference held in Richmond, Virginia. Yet I wonder how many really heard me.

WHAT YOU NEED TO KNOW BEFORE YOU EVEN THINK ABOUT TRADING THE FOREX

Only a few years ago, most people had never even heard of trading the foreign currency exchange (also known as the forex). Even now, many have never heard of it. But so much information is available on the Internet that if you've heard or seen the term, all you have to do is simply type it in a search engine and a mass of information is available for free—though that information can be bad or good, misleading or correct. In writing this book, my goal is to provide *accurate and useful information* about how to trade the forex.

During the early stages of the forex, traders who wanted to participate were required to post quite a bit of money with a brokerage, bank, or trading firm. Today, however, if you want to trade the forex, you can trade mini accounts, also known as dollar accounts. Moreover, you can open these mini accounts with as little as $250 USA to have a taste of what it's like to trade live—which allows you to test the emotional side of trading as well before you make a decision to pursue an exciting day trading career. These dollar accounts (currencies will be referred to as USD from this point forward) allow you to earn or lose approximately $1 USD per point (called a *pip*) per contract (called a *lot*). If you're successful and you develop some confidence in your trading ability, you may even open a standard account with brokers and participate with the big guys, such as banks and other institutional groups, at an average of $10 USD per point per contract.

LEARN FROM A CERTIFIED MENTOR

So how can you learn to trade the forex? Most new traders begin learning on their own through a trial-and-error process of wins and losses, while probably gathering general information on the Internet or at the library. However, this is probably *not* the best approach to take.

Instead, I recommend having a certified forex mentor, which may be the best avenue available to you. It may take a couple of days for a mentor just to walk you through basic procedures and working assignments, but these will help you along the way to success, whether you have experience trading or not. Once you've learned the basic techniques and procedures, then, as a new forex trader, your primary focus should be to work on your attitude, discipline, and skill development. This takes time, patience, and maybe even some prayer along the way.

To clearly understand all of the conceptual procedures found within this book (which includes the S90/Crossover as well as several ongoing applications), I suggest you learn the basics of forex trading skills along with other intermediate and advanced methodologies from a certified mentor.

What is a certified mentor? A certified mentor is a successful trader who (1) has been formally trained, (2) has produced proven documented trading results, and (3) attends continuing education sessions that are required by monitoring groups such as the Independent Forex Traders Association (IFxTA) or the Concorde Foundation. This type of independent governing agency monitors registered mentors to make sure they are current and in good standing with the most up-to-date research and methodology available to traders. These nonprofit organizations may also provide legal representation to traders who are dues-paying members of the association should the trader have issues with a registered broker or bank regarding a trading discrepancy. They also monitor and police registered mentors to ensure quality—for example, by issuing a mentorship cease-and-desist order against violators.

Alert: To clearly understand the methodology described in this book, it will be helpful for you to have a basic understanding of how to determine trends, resistances, supports, and confirming procedures, using software that utilizes River Oscillator Indicator

(ROI), River Channel (RC), River Channel Up/River Channel Down (RCU/RCD), and their extensions with cluster formations for possible reversal entries. A brief and simple explanation of each of these subjects is provided when each is first mentioned in the book. I also recommend you learn the correct procedures for understanding the first two tiers of the legal and illegal elements of S90/Crossovers, because this knowledge will help you interpret the extreme levels and their off-market Fibonacci layers as well as the overlapping Fibonaccis, which will be explained briefly in future chapters.

HOW THIS BOOK CAN HELP YOU

To reiterate a point I made in the Introduction, this book is for traders—whether you're advanced or just a beginner—who need something simple and reliable regarding a trade entry that will produce profits in the majority of trade entries. The book's goal is to help you in the following ways:

- To possibly supplement your personal income with a simple trade.
- To help you develop personal trading skills.
- To help you become a professional full-time trader eventually, if you so desire.

The S90/Crossovers and extreme levels of the market are not the only methodologies that produce profits, but they may be the simplest and most reliable approaches to learn how to trade the forex with consistency. Some who use the system have produced 50, 100, 200, and even 400 or more trades in a row without a loss.*

---

*__Disclaimer:__ Trading the foreign exchange market carries a high level of risk and may not be suitable for all investors. Before deciding to trade the foreign exchange market, you should carefully consider your investment objectives, level of experience, and risk appetite. The possibility exists that you could sustain a loss of some or all of your initial investment; therefore, you should not invest money that you cannot afford to lose. You should be aware of all the risk associated with foreign currency exchange trading, and you should seek advice from an independent financial advisor if you have any doubts.

CHAPTER 2

Modernist versus Traditionalist Approaches to Trading

Modernism and traditionalism as well as the various trading styles and methodologies found within the markets are things that every trader should understand and appreciate. Modernism (as I use the term in this book) is related to proprietary systems used for trading, in contrast to traditionalism, which is based on traditional approaches used in trading smaller markets within the trading industry.

I hope you will understand there is a difference between modern and traditional systems and will explore the difference with an open mind. In general, I've found that learning something about the history of the forex, as well as a few of the different types of traditional signals, trading styles, and other concepts (information that is available to everyone for free or for a fee) helps you see the significance of trading the larger forex market while using proprietary tools instead of traditional software. This requires just a little personal research. After you learn the basics from this book, and after you develop a personal awareness about the largest financial industry in the world, your eyes should be open to the possibility of becoming a *professional* trader or, if you're already trading, to becoming a *better* trader.

I must give credit to those who early on forged the way with research and development, often by trial and error. These traditionalists made it possible for everyone to enjoy the opportunity that the forex market presents today. Experimenting and seeking the secrets of success should never be ignored. Many traditional traders from Wall Street are the unsung heroes of the trading industry—as well as those who filed for bankruptcy along the way while looking to find the secret of perfected entries, stops, and limits.

In addition, there are others who had large amounts of money, which gave them the power to stay in the market: They made fortunes without much focus on either the technical approach or the fundamental approach to the markets. George Soros stated in one of his books that to be successful in the forex, a trader must have "sustaining power," meaning enough money to survive market swings; many traditional traders became swing traders while not using stops. When the market moved against these traders, their hope was that the market would eventually come back to profits; and often it did. However, when losses did occur, the damage to margins was often so severe that some traders had to quit the industry.

With the advancement of technology and continued research into the market recently, Mr. Soros's theory may not be true any longer. With a little research, you may find that some very famous traders and authors have either filed for bankruptcy or left the market with ongoing failures because they would not consider evaluating new, proven concepts and methodologies that have been developed.

There are many newly developed trading procedures and strategies available now in the marketplace. Traders new to the industry must remember that *success comes only with effort.* Many market explorers, research technicians, and traders have quit (or even passed away) just before success might have been reached. When I began trading, I reminded myself of how Thomas Edison struggled in the beginning of his most successful venture. When developing the lightbulb, he continued to forge forward, at great expense, attempting more than 1,000 (some say 10,000) time-consuming experiments before achieving success. I also thought of the cheetah, which has been tracked at running nearly 80 miles per hour but nevertheless has to make an average of 100 attempts to kill one antelope for dinner. One success out of an average 100 attempts would discourage any new trader if this were the case in the market!

Many beginning traders experience losses just before achieving success, and most will give up trading with a bad attitude toward the industry or, worse yet, toward their mentor. I have met traders who believe that their failure means that someone else must be to blame, yet these same traders will always accept success and forget their guiding mentors. If you cannot be responsible for your actions in the market, you should never trade the forex. Jim Rohn, a famous speaker and author, once said that most issues regarding failure are found between the ears.

I would suggest you keep an open mind to traditional trading styles, but also be open to the new systems and procedures that are developed every year to accommodate market conditions that seem to be changing constantly as the industry grows. Successful trading requires ongoing research and development, which only a few companies in the world are willing to share with the average everyday trader. If you're new to the forex industry, it would be a good idea for you to consider locating a mentorship company that has a proven track record of success for personalized help as well as ongoing research. If you're considering a mentor program, keep in mind that it is also helpful to have a development program in place to help you with support after you complete your initial mentoring session. If you are a beginning trader who is self-trained in the forex—and even if you have previous trading experience in traditional markets (e.g., futures, stocks, etc.)—your losses in the forex will most likely far outweigh the cost you would have paid for professional help.

"Some are meant to play the game, and then there are those who must teach." Can this be true? What's wrong with learning from a mentor who actually trades full-time for a living? Unfortunately, most mentors do not trade successfully, but those who do are more than willing to be certified properly. A *certified* mentor is more than willing to provide ongoing copies of his or her personal trading history as proof to a nonprejudiced third-party mediation group; as an alternate suggestion, mentors could submit instant notification to their traders as well as to the mediation group of personal live trade entries as they happen for a limited time period. This type of proof would justify the mentor's or author's credibility.

SOMETHING TO THINK ABOUT REGARDING THE HISTORY OF THE FOREX

Everyone associated with the forex currency exchange has opinions of how the forex began, and extensive information is found all over the Internet. Since the forex has evolved into the largest financial industry in the world, the daily opportunity to become involved with it has created unbelievable growth within the exchange, which averages $2.2 trillion (as of July 2005) with surges in the market toward $6.5 trillion at times. During a banking symposium held in New York City in July 2006 (sponsored by the *FXWeekly* group), it was announced that the daily volume of the forex had increased to an amount in excess of $3 trillion per day. This per-day volume of the forex is much larger than the volumes of traditional trading industries such as the stock market, which is, as of 2007, currently averaging approximately $17 billion per day of volume. For that matter, the forex is greater than all other markets, including the legal and illegal drug industry. The industry continues to grow regardless of the number of new traders, fund managers, and firms that are seeking wealth or increased profits on their investments. Even with the 80 percent failure rate that most authors claim exist within the forex, the industry continues to grow every year.

It is my thought that maybe there were seeds planted long before the arrival of computers when trading in large quantities began appearing during the days of Solomon, as found in the number-one best-selling, most distributed book in the world, the Bible. Solomon opened many doors of trade and exchange without the influence of computers, data feeds, news announcements, political secrets, and spontaneous fundamental announcements. He was able to accumulate wealth that even modern-day traders haven't been able to match. Although Solomon had to use caravans moving very slowly to transport products from one geographical region to other regions, the basic trading industry most likely grew then as it continues to grow even today. Regarding commodities, futures, gold exchange, and so on, Solomon probably did more for the trading industry, especially futures in grains, cloth, corn, wheat, and other needed tangible and intangible products, than anyone will ever imagine.

As time passed and verbal exchanges became available in market facilities such as those on Wall Street, where the high volatility of the market exchange created quick profits that made many wealthy, the market began to grow and continues at an even higher rate. The forerunner of the New York Stock Exchange on Wall Street was founded in 1792. Traders with large amounts of funds for hedging could sustain their existence in the market with lower risk, while those with larger or smaller margins (but with less industry intelligence) gave up their trade exchanges with losses.

It was a battle of the bulls against the bears as systems, theories, and methodologies began to emerge; traders began to pay fees for personalized mentorship in hopes of finding the secret grail to successful and consistent trading results. Many types of how-to systems began to develop as a result of positive trading, while poor trading results could have affected the growth of mentorship programs as well. Today, you can find (and in large quantities) numerous books, specialized software, proprietary systems, entry procedures, forex investment counselors, trading videos, multilevel deals, and the list goes on.

Furthermore, many new branches within the industry are constantly evolving as legitimate systems and procedures of methodology. Often, though, you will find that mentors and authors do not even trade and obscure their inefficient trading abilities or lack of success by running everyone else down but never proving their own personal ability as traders. They make their livings from selling systems and books; therefore, I suggest you avoid them and instead (and as I mentioned in the Introduction) find a certified mentor.

MILLION-DOLLAR TIP

It is important to study only with someone who walks the talk (i.e., a certified mentor) when attempting to develop personal trading skills in the forex.

I suggest you reread the last statement, because it is true; this million-dollar tip will keep you, as a new forex trader, from making a serious mistake when you select a mentor to guide you in trading the forex.

CHAPTER 3

What Is an S90/Crossover and How Was It Discovered?

In 1997, I took a forex course from an individual who understood the mathematical and traditional concepts of the forex like no one else I have ever met. I paid $10,000 for the private session. Everything he said impressed me, because I knew absolutely nothing about the forex at that time. The two-day seminar was conducted by book only and involved a lot of mathematical concepts and formulas that I had never heard of before in my life.

During the first three hours of the seminar, the complexity of the material was simply too much for my mind to accept. When my mind did clear up occasionally, all I could focus on was the fact that I had paid $10,000 for the course. I spent most of the first morning trying to figure out how to ask for the nonrefundable fee back. I was also trying to figure out how I was going to tell my family that I had just given a cashier's check for $10,000 to a total stranger for a training seminar about a product called the forex that no one I knew had ever even heard of.

After the first three hours, I went to lunch and prayed. Afterward, I felt more relaxed and at ease with my situation. I laughed at almost everything that was said during the rest of the two-day seminar. The instructor didn't speak very good English, and I guess my laughter and smiles made him think I was just enjoying the class.

About three months later I attended another course, this one taught by someone in Florida who at least spoke English, but I never told the Florida mentor that I had already been introduced to the forex. I just listened and became aware that I had actually picked up some tips and methodology from the first mentor. Having the information repeated into my brain by someone else may have been why I understood the second session more than the first.

I continued taking courses, eventually working with a total of seven mentors during my initial days as a neophyte trader. All of them taught me something. I felt every class was worth what I paid, even though I didn't make any money as a trader until after I had paid my dues with time and a lot of patience.

The only mentor who would continue to communicate with me, for a fee, was in Europe. He attempted to answer 100 percent of my questions by e-mail. He charged me per e-mail, which made me not repeat my questions and caused me to be very selective with the questions that I sent him to answer.

I found out later that only three of my seven mentors were actually trading live in the markets. Several of my former mentors were living off the mentorship fees instead of personally trading. I now consider this very offensive to any new trader being introduced to the forex. No mentor is worth paying for if he or she is not currently—and successfully—trading live.

Whether because of my confusion due to way too much knowledge or maybe an unexplained emotional drawdown, my losses were incredibly large in the beginning. However, one day, after suffering incredibly large losses, I had a dream and saw the details of something in the markets that had always been present. After months of research, it became apparent to me that no one else had ever seen this signal procedure or pattern in the markets before, either.

This research led me to the S90/Crossover. I have always felt this dream was a gift from God that had to be shared with everyone. So, once a trader has learned the language from a certified mentor, I will continue to share with all new forex students features and application procedures for free. I will continue to offer free help for as long as I am able.

The only requirement to understand the S90/Crossover is for you to use a candlestick charting service that has a River Oscillator Indicator (ROI) trading oscillator, a Fibonacci level indicator, and a line drawing tool. The different levels of the S90/Crossover have more value and accuracy if the data feed is from the averages of more than 100 data banks, which may consist of clearing firms such as future commodity merchants, institutions, and banks that are willing to participate in the clearing of trades. For every buyer there must be a seller (and vice versa) and large financial organizations provide this liquidity along with individual traders worldwide. Currently, I use a charting service that has, at times, more than 500 data banks of combined data feed with averaged streaming real-time data, which then produces a modified average to measure the currency market properly.

The S90/Crossover is made of both resistances and supports found within uptrends and downtrends. The resistances later become support targets, and support levels later become resistance targets—provided that certain criteria are met. The S90/Crossover levels also provide proper planning opportunities for exact entry points and exits. Once you learn how accurate these levels are, they become a free source of information for you that you can use with any charting service. Free is a good thing!

Since the night of the dream, I have taught many traders the first two levels of the signal; however, there are four levels to the S90/Crossover procedure. The chapters that follow present the first two levels, as well as information regarding the associated extreme levels of the S90/Crossover, which I often use as entries as well as for profit targets. The last two levels are a bit more complicated, and I suggest, once again, to locate a certified mentor who has been properly trained to explain the more advanced levels of the S90/Crossover. You can find contact information for a certified mentor in the Resources section of this book.

MILLION-DOLLAR TIP

The S90/Crossover has a foundation based on historical resistance and support points within a trading range. There are legal and illegal features found on the first two levels of the signal, which allow you to enter on valid signals and avoid entries that only look good by observing the illegal features.

LET'S GET STARTED: USING CANDLESTICK CHARTS

For the purposes of the following explanations, Japanese candlestick charts will be used to illustrate the S90/Crossovers. At one time in history, the Japanese actually measured grain and other commodities using real candlesticks. When computers and charting software applications began appearing throughout the world, candlestick software was developed and then used to measure the massive data feeds as well. Candlestick charting is used by many traders to help measure market momentum; for the sake of illustration, many candlestick time compression charts will be used to illustrate and compare how the S90/Crossovers are interpreted.

There are many other types of charting applications to measure the markets, such as bar, scatter, line, and wave charts. Any charting service will do, but for simplicity, only candlestick applications are illustrated in this book.

RESISTANCE IDENTIFICATION IN TRADING RANGES WITH NEWLY FORMING RESISTANCES

Resistances, for the purpose and application of the S90/Crossover within a bear trading range, are indicated by a grouping of five (or more) candlestick bodies with the center wick(s) being higher than the tops of the two candle bodies or wicks that have previously formed to the left and the two that subsequently form to the right. See Figure 3.1.

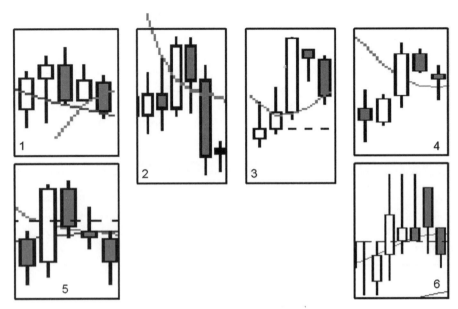

FIGURE 3.1 Examples of resistance points.
Courtesy of Concorde Forex Group, Inc.

Each of the six candlestick charts shown in Figure 3.1 is an example of a resistance point. Chart 2 in Figure 3.1 is referred to as "twins," because the high point of the resistance point has two candles with the same high (top of wick); this is a resistance because it has two candles to the left and two candles to the right that are lower than the tops of the two twin candles. Chart 6 in Figure 3.1 is also a resistance point; it is referred to as "triplets."

As the market moves down, resistances are developed, and they should be marked as illustrated in Figure 3.2, in case the market returns to that level. The circled top and bottom represent the trading range in question. Notice that the support areas of the trading range are not considered to have value within the range; therefore, no lines are drawn for supports. Supports will be illustrated later in this chapter.

Figure 3.3 shows a downward trading range with resistances indicated on the top side of the trading range, which is the beginning of the search for a S90/Crossover.

As the market pierces the horizontal line B, a stall often happens in the market, and one of four features will be observed:

1. If the market arrives to the level but does not breach the level with an open and close of a candle body, it may go sideways until it either breaches the level and continues in the same direction or reverses and returns later if the level was not breached (again, see Figure 3.3).

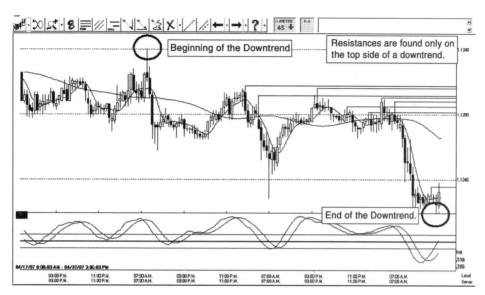

FIGURE 3.2 Example of marking resistance levels in a downtrend.
Courtesy of Concorde Forex Group, Inc.

FIGURE 3.3 Resistances in a downtrend.
Courtesy of Concorde Forex Group, Inc.

2. The market may strike the level and a reversal may occur, depending on whether the level was also duplicated as a Fibonacci level. As long as the level is not breached with an open and close of a candle body, then the odds are increased that the market will eventually return to the level. If the level becomes a future Fibonacci level within a future trading range, then the odds of the target level being reached are increased tremendously.

In summary, the farther away from the level that the market moves, the greater profits may be made when the market begins its move back toward the S90/Crossover level, which has been duplicated with a new trading range Fibonacci level. Figure 3.4 illustrates this.

3. The market could breach the level with an open and a close as it passes by the level and then retreats back to the opposite side for a new open and close. This means that the market has opened and closed on each side of the level and the level can never be trusted again, unless it forms a new support or resistance in the future in the same area, which increases its value at that time. (See Figure 3.5.) This type of market action on each side of the level is considered an illegal S90/Crossover and cannot be trusted unless a future level is established in the same area with a new trading range. Then it becomes a historical level with increased odds of becoming

FIGURE 3.4 Example of the market returning to the resistance level, followed by a reversal. Courtesy of Concorde Forex Group, Inc.

FIGURE 3.5 Example of an illegal S90/Crossover.
Courtesy of Concorde Forex Group, Inc.

a market attraction for a future target or a bounce entry as a reversal point in the market.

4. If the market not only breaches the level, as shown in Figure 3.6, but immediately continues in the direction of the former run, then this is a good sign, and as long as the level is not defined as illegal, the odds have increased that the market will eventually return to the crossover as a target and a possible new bounce entry, provided other confirmations are present to justify the entry. Such bounce confirmations may be a PCI (percentage change indicator), ROI, or even a volume indicator. This new entry would be considered a reversal or bounce entry.

TRADING RANGES WITH NEWLY FORMING SUPPORTS

Supports within a bull trading range, much like the resistances in a bear trading range, are also indicated by a minimum grouping of five candlestick bodies with the center candle(s) or wick(s) being lower than the bottoms of the two candles to the left and to the right, as shown in Figure 3.7. Notice that the resistances are not considered at this level to have value within the range. As the market moves upward, the supports should be marked, as illustrated in Figure 3.8, in case the market returns to that level. Figure 3.7 offers an example of a view of how supports will appear.

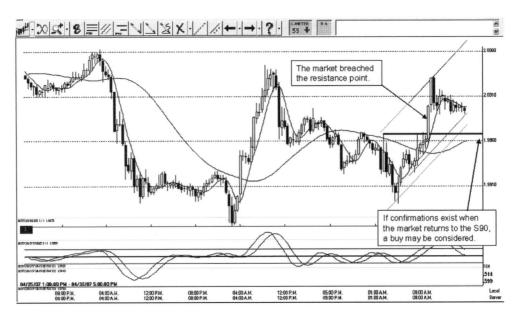

FIGURE 3.6 Example of the market breaching the resistance level and continuing in the direction of the former run.
Courtesy of Concorde Forex Group, Inc.

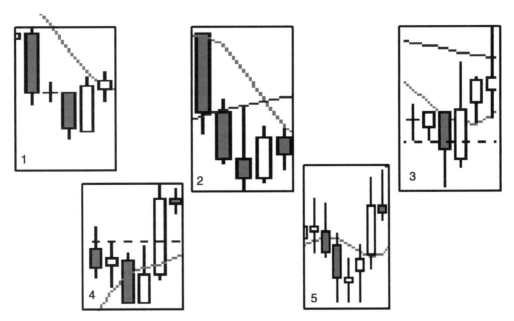

FIGURE 3.7 Examples of support points.
Courtesy of Concorde Forex Group, Inc.

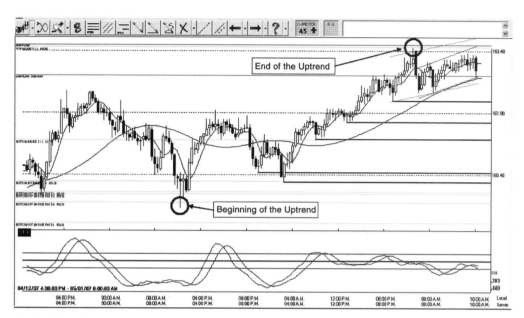

FIGURE 3.8 Example of marking support levels in an uptrend.
Courtesy of Concorde Forex Group, Inc.

SUPPORT IDENTIFICATION REITERATED

Trading ranges with newly forming supports, for the purpose and application of the S90/Crossover within a bull trading range, are indicated by a grouping of five or more candlestick bodies with the center wick(s) being lower than the bottoms of the two candle bodies or wicks that have previously formed to the left and the two that subsequently form to the right. Notice that the resistance areas of the trading range are not considered at this level to have value within the range and therefore no arrows are drawn on the top side of the trend within the illustration in Figure 3.9. When the market is bullish, then we look for supports to mark within the bullish trading range. As the market moves up, supports are developed, and they should be marked as illustrated in Figure 3.9 (i.e., on the bottom side of the trend) in case the market returns to the level.

Just as covered previously on the resistance development side of the S90/Crossover, if the movement of the currency pierces the horizontal line, a stall often happens in the market, and one of four features will be observed:

First, if the market arrives to the S90/Crossover level but does not breach the level with an open and close of a candle body, it may go sideways and eventually either breach the level and continue in the same direction or reverse and return later if the level was not breached. (See Figure 3.10.)

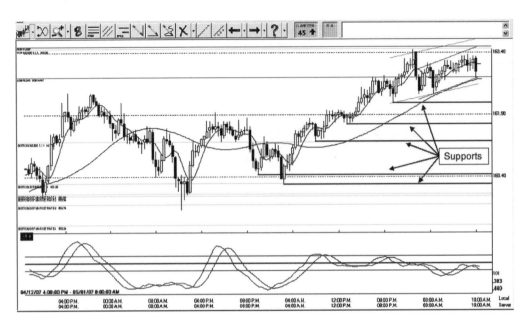

FIGURE 3.9 Example of marking support levels in a bullish market.
Courtesy of Concorde Forex Group, Inc.

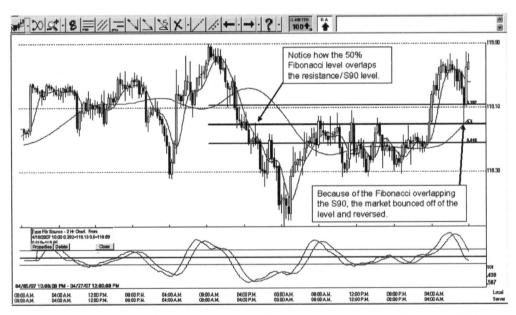

FIGURE 3.10 Example of a sideways pattern followed by a market reversal from the S90 level.
Courtesy of Concorde Forex Group, Inc.

Second, if the market strikes the support level and reverses, it may depend on whether the level was also duplicated as a Fibonacci level. A Fibonacci level in this scenario is drawn from the previous trading range in question and may be indicated by a .50, .382, .618, or another Fibonacci number. (If you need more information on Fibonacci levels, check the Internet; there are also many books available on this topic.) As long as the level is not breached with an open and close of a candle body, then the odds are increased that the market will eventually return to the same support level. If this particular level becomes a future Fibonacci level within a future trading range, then the odds of the target level being reached are increased tremendously.

Summary: The farther away from the resistance or support horizontal level that the market moves, if the market remains legal, the greater the profits that can be made when the market begins its move back toward the S90/Crossover level. If that level happens to coincide with a Fibonacci level due to the development of a new trading range, then the strength of the level becomes more obvious. (See Figure 3.11.)

Third, the market could breach the exact level with an open and close as it passes by the level and then retreats back to the opposite side for a new open and close. This means that the market has opened and closed on each side of the level and the level can never be trusted again, unless it forms a new support or resistance in the future in the same area, give or take 10 pips, which increases its value at that time. (For the sake of

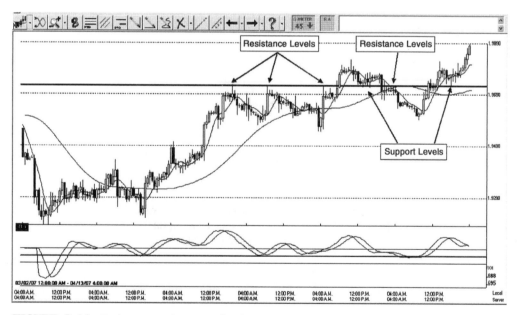

FIGURE 3.11 Resistance and support levels.
Courtesy of Concorde Forex Group, Inc.

simplicity and clarity, when a historical event such as a repetitive level occurs, the word *area* may be used in association with a historical S90/Crossover level, which means "give or take 10 pips on either side of the level.")

In general, once the S90/Crossover becomes illegal and the same level keeps recurring in the same approximate area, then you should take notice of the validity and strength regarding the importance of the area for a reversal entry or a future target if trading toward the historical area. Most likely, if this type of event is occurring, a Fibonacci level will be in place as well for additional confirmations. To reiterate a comment made earlier about not trusting the level if an open and close occurs on each side of the S90/Crossover, this type of market action on each side of the level is considered an illegal S90/Crossover and cannot be trusted again unless a future level is established in the same area with a new trading range. Then it becomes a historical level with increased odds of becoming a market attraction for a future target or a bounce entry as a reversal point in the market.

Figure 3.12 is an example of a resistance point turning into an S90.

Figure 3.13 is an example of a support point turning into an S90.

Figure 3.14 is an example of when a resistance S90 becomes illegal.

Figure 3.15 is an example of when a support S90 becomes illegal.

Fourth, as in earlier illustrations based on supports of a trading range that generated an S90/Crossover, the market not only may breach the level, but may immediately continue in the direction of the former run. This is a good sign as long as the level is not

Open and close above a resistance line equals …
Validated S90/Crossover

FIGURE 3.12 Example of a resistance point turning into an S90.
Courtesy of Concorde Forex Group, Inc.

FIGURE 3.13 Example of a support point turning into an S90. Courtesy of Concorde Forex Group, Inc.

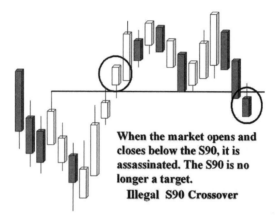

FIGURE 3.14 Example of when a resistance S90 becomes illegal. Courtesy of Concorde Forex Group, Inc.

FIGURE 3.15 Example of when a support S90 becomes illegal. Courtesy of Concorde Forex Group, Inc.

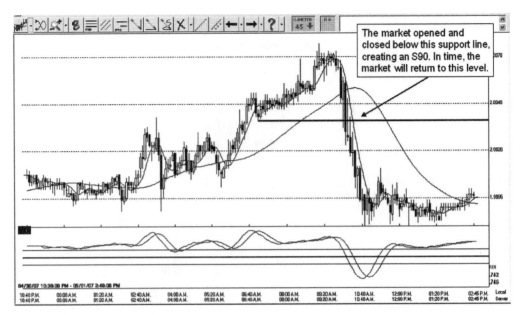

The market opened and closed below this support line, creating an S90. In time, the market will return to this level.

FIGURE 3.16 Example of the market breaching the support line.
Courtesy of Concorde Forex Group, Inc.

defined as illegal. The odds are the market will eventually return to the crossover as a target and a possible new bounce entry may become evident, provided other confirmations are present to justify the entry. Such bounce confirmations may be a PCI, a ROI, and a historical S90/Crossover, which are often referred to as clusters in the market, or even traditional volume indicators of some type. This new entry would be considered a reversal or bounce entry. (See Figure 3.16.)

BREACHING A LINE LEGALLY OR ILLEGALLY

An S90/Crossover begins with resistances or supports. An extended resistance or support line is drawn horizontally into the future. The market may return to the horizontal line, and at the point of contact a new predictable future is determined. This determination is based on whether the line is breached. This is also where the illegal or legal aspect of the level is determined.

Figure 3.17 is an illustration of a support line breach. In Figure 3.18, the market has opened and closed below the support line, turning it into a legal S90.

Figure 3.19 is an illustration of an *illegal* breach.

FIGURE 3.17 Illustration of a support line breach.
Courtesy of Concorde Forex Group, Inc.

FIGURE 3.18 Illustration of a legal breach.
Courtesy of Concorde Forex Group, Inc.

The S90 is now an illegal S90 because the market has opened and closed on both sides. This level is no longer trustworthy. The market needs to create a new S90 in order for a trader to trust the market to return to that level.

FIGURE 3.19 Illustration of an illegal breach.
Courtesy of Concorde Forex Group, Inc.

.25 (Chin)   .382 (Chest)   .50 (Waist)   .618 (Knee)   .75 (Ankle)

FIGURE 3.20 Resistance levels are found on the top side of a bear trading range.
Courtesy of Concorde Forex Group, Inc.

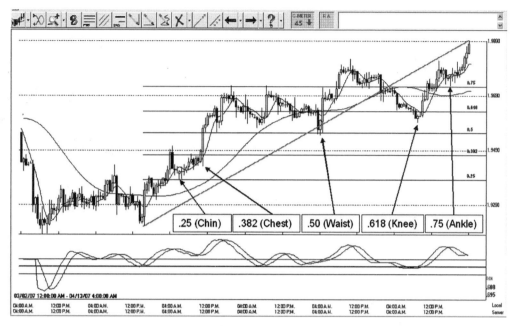

FIGURE 3.21 Support levels are found on the bottom side of a bull trading range. Courtesy of Concorde Forex Group, Inc.

APPLYING FIBONACCI LEVELS

The Fibonacci .50 area of a trading range may offer an S90/Crossover support or resistance for the birth of a new future entry or target, depending on whether the future contact level is breached legally. If the level is a Fib level, then its strength increases. The five levels of a trading range that have increased sensitivity are 25 percent, 38.2 percent, 50 percent, 61.8 percent, and 75 percent of the measured range.

Resistance and support levels, or S90/Crossover birth levels, may coincidentally occur at the levels shown in Figures 3.20 and 3.21. If you do not understand how Fibonacci levels are derived, you might remember them better by associating the most common Fib levels of a trading range with the human body, which also offers Fibonacci levels. For example, the chest area is .382, the waist is .50, and the knees represent the .618 level of the body, as shown in Figures 3.20 and 3.21.

CHAPTER 4

Developing the Profit Targets or Entry Points of a Trading Range for the S90/Crossover

The S90/Crossover has levels within a trading range that may or may not be associated with Fibonacci levels. As stated in Chapter 3, the S90/Crossover begins with either supports on the bottom side of an uptrend trading range or resistance areas on the top side of a downtrend.

EXPLANATION OF LEVELS AND HOW THEY MAY BE INTERPRETED

Although all levels must be considered for targets and reversals, there are certain levels that have more importance than others. For example, in Table 4.1, the levels illustrate the number of S90/Crossovers that occurred during just one New York open. Notice that one level is duplicated on the different time compressions. The level 1.2809, which is highlighted in Table 4.1, is common from the five-minute time compression through the four-hour time compression, but it is not recognized on the daily or weekly chart. This level is a prime level for a reversal, provided that either traditional or modernistic signals are triggered. If signals are triggered toward the levels with proper confirmations, then the 1.2809 level would be interpreted as a possible target. If the market strikes that level and other confirmations are present for a reversal, then that level should generate safety for a bounce-type trade entry.

TABLE 4.1		S90/Crossovers during Various Time Compressions in an Uptrend						
5MIN UPTREND	10MIN UPTREND	30MIN UPTREND	60MIN UPTREND	2HR UPTREND	4HR UPTREND	DY UPTREND	WK UPTREND
1.2842	1.2834	1.2834	1.2834	**1.2809**	**1.2809**		
1.2838	1.2828	1.2828	**1.2809**	1.2702	1.2702		
1.2828	1.2811	**1.2809**					
1.2817	**1.2809**						
1.2811	1.2764						
1.2809	1.2736						
1.2764	1.2872						
1.2759	1.2820						
1.2677							
1.2672							

S90/CROSSOVER LEVELS ARE NOT THE SAME AS A PIVOT POINT

Although the S90/Crossover levels appear to be similar to traditional pivot points, they are not. Pivot points are generally known as levels of possible reversal entry points as well as profit targets. Although pivot points are awesome at times, the problem I have observed is that they are published on the Internet and may give clearing firms and banks the opportunity to herd traders into a position of taking massive stops from smaller traders. This may be considered swimming with the sharks, so to speak. These S90/Crossovers may sometimes, by coincidence, appear at the same level as a pivot point, but they are more consistent for reversals or targets, even during conflicting seasonal market times. Many traditional traders feel that the market is seasonal and therefore a signal that works this season may not work the next season. For example, in July 2006 many pivot traders suffered great losses, while those who understood how to accurately predict S90/Crossovers were able to avoid losses during this same time period.

I have a low opinion of pivot points, because they are published on the Internet where thousands of traders may trade them. It is very likely that traders follow daily pivot publications like sheep to the slaughter. They often have temporary wins, which build confidence, but then suddenly these traders with almost identical protective stops are taken out by the thousands by only one or two pips. It has been said by very famous authors and professional traders that trading with the crowd will ultimately lead to disaster, and it often seems that those who trade pivots eventually disappear from the market unless they have great sustaining power. To make profits in the market, you must learn to trade against the crowd. I believe that when the market direction is confirmed by River

Oscillator Indicator (ROI) oscillators, the S90/Crossover will help you trade against the crowd with success.

S-90 CROSSOVERS WITHIN A RANGE

Table 4.1 represents a trading range comprised of supports on the bottom side of an uptrend that is made up of previous historical S90/Crossovers within an approximate 200-pip trading range.

Educational Note: A gap present on an S90/Crossover increases the odds of success as a profit target and also as a new reversal entry. S90/Crossovers that occur in conjunction with a larger compression trend will also indicate a strong level for reversals or targets—provided additional confirmations exist to justify the entry. Also, when one level, as listed in Table 4.1, is found on numerous time compressions, this strengthens its value within a trading range for a future reversal entry or a profit target if trading toward the duplicated level. It may often become a former historical S90/Crossover level where the level has been revived and duplicated. To reiterate the concept for clarity, this type of market development allows the duplicated level to become a stronger area for profit targets and also possible new reversal entries at the time of the strike.

Table 4.2 illustrates the levels that had appeared only on smaller time compressions, while larger compressions had no agreements in place. Only two time compressions were duplicated on the bear side of the markets. During this period of time, the market was in an overall uptrend, and therefore more S90/Crossovers appeared, as illustrated in Table 4.2. Should the market change direction and develop a new downtrend, then more new S90/Crossovers will gradually develop to match the larger S90/Crossover levels shown in Table 4.2. Currently, no larger compressions have duplicated levels in Table 4.2.

TABLE 4.2 S90/Crossovers during Various Time Compressions in a Downtrend

5MIN DNTREND	10MIN DNTREND	30MIN DNTREND	60MIN DNTREND	2HR DNTREND	4HR DNTREND	DY DNTREND	WK DNTREND
		1.2504	1.2503	1.2472	1.2470	1.1758	1.1932
		1.2470	**1.2465**	1.2464	1.2429	1.1622	1.1552
		1.2465	1.2350	1.2282	**1.1822**	1.1430	0.9378
		1.2422	1.2338	1.2125	1.1468	1.1322	
			1.2281	1.1941	1.1322	1.0143	
				1.1822	1.1112	1.1018	
				1.1538		0.0895	
				1.1528		0.8916	
				1.1468		0.8858	

All of the levels shown in Table 4.2 were identified as legal crossovers (LCs) and must be respected as potential reversal levels if additional confirmations exist at the time of level arrivals. Notice the one duplicated level, which is a historical S90/Crossover area, but is also duplicated on other time compressions.

The reason that both uptrend and downtrend crossovers are listed in both Tables 4.1 and 4.2 is because crossovers may occur at the same time in both directions within the trending time compressions. Remember, trends within trends occur at the same time, depending on the time compression size that you're observing. This sounds like an oxymoron, so here's an explanation: The five-minute time compression may show that an immediate downtrend is in progress, while the two-hour time compression has the appearance of an immediate uptrend, and the weekly is in an uptrend or a downtrend. The point is that not all time compressions may agree with each other at the same time regarding direction. Remember, it takes 2,016 five-minute candlesticks to form just one weekly candlestick. This means that with smaller time compressions, there may be a lot of trend activity with up or down directions going on while larger compressions may not acknowledge the activity of smaller compressions.

Trading ranges seem to change almost daily due to constantly changing market conditions. In any trading range—whether in 1–, 5–, 10–, or 30+–minute time compressions—the Fibonacci levels found within all trading ranges are known to be measured into infinity. If this is true, then would it not be true that pivot points and Fibonacci levels would occur in such massive numbers that you would be confused as to which level is the most important? This is the problem with pivots: Most traders cannot figure out which pivot is telling the truth. If an S90/Crossover just happens to be on the same pivot point, then you have a combination that produces a very strong level for targets or reversals.

When the legal S90/Crossover is combined with confirming signals from a legal gap, a trend wall, Fibonacci clusters, or an overlapping Fibonacci level, it becomes a powerful reversal point for an entry or a target to trade toward. An explanation of the previously mentioned confirming signals will be explored along with the applications in future chapters.

LEGAL AND ILLEGAL S90/CROSSOVERS

A legal crossover (LC) is a visual confirmation that you must observe to determine if a future profit strike or entry will be valid. These LCs occur every day in different currency combinations, and you should mark those LCs that can be trusted on charts immediately for future reference. Legal crossovers can be trusted in the market, and illegal crossovers cannot be trusted. Often, illegal crossovers are interpreted by many traders who use traditional signals such as pivots as an entry, frequently causing losses. Legal crossovers usually are not associated with a traditional signal, and if they do appear at approximately the same level, then it is most likely a coincidence.

Many traders never understand the methodology of the S90/Crossover and therefore, without the help of proper data feed and software that identify ongoing fresh S90/Crossovers, the methodology may be useless. Two companies, Concorde Forex Group, Inc. (CFG) and Forex Producers Group, LLC (FP), now offer software for traders to view the S90/Crossovers that have the most significance for identifying in advance the most probable trading ranges on most currency combinations. When historical S90/Crossovers are bunched together as clusters, they become very powerful target confirmations as well as exit points in the market. These historical S90/Crossovers are also possible reversal entry points.

The simplest application is to consider the S90/Crossovers on the first two levels as possible targets to trade toward or for reversal entries once the levels have been reached. The key is to have multiple time compression or trend wall clashes for possible market reversals as confirmations before entering the market.

Trend walls that have a clashing point with an S90/Crossover that happens to be relatively close to or exactly lines up with a horizontal extreme level will usually have other indicators also implying a reversal in the market.

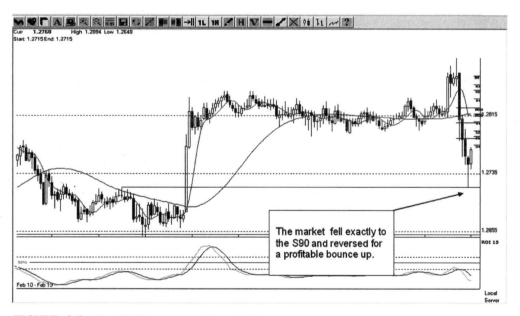

FIGURE 4.1 The S90/Crossover strike at its best.
Courtesy of Concorde Forex Group, Inc.

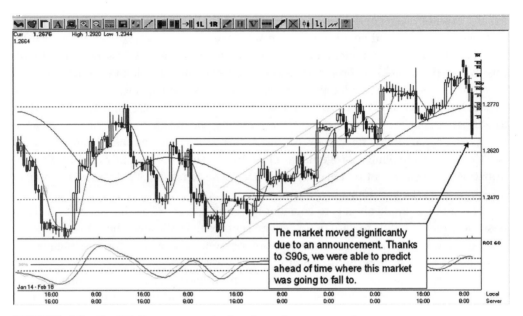

The market moved significantly due to an announcement. Thanks to S90s, we were able to predict ahead of time where this market was going to fall to.

FIGURE 4.2 The S90/Crossover on the four-hour time compression.
Courtesy of Concorde Forex Group, Inc.

The market fell right to the two-hour S90 level. Since this S90 was legal on multiple compressions, it turned into a stronger level. The market moved up approximately 150 pips.

FIGURE 4.3 The S90/Crossover on the two-hour time compression.
Courtesy of Concorde Forex Group, Inc.

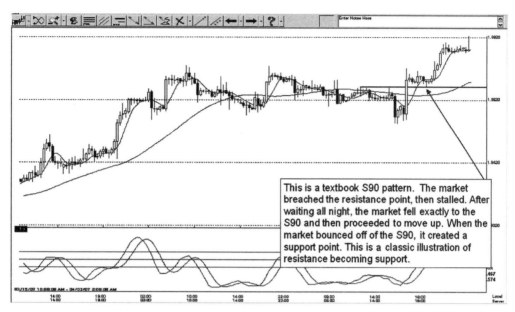

This is a textbook S90 pattern. The market breached the resistance point, then stalled. After waiting all night, the market fell exactly to the S90 and then proceeded to move up. When the market bounced off of the S90, it created a support point. This is a classic illustration of resistance becoming support.

FIGURE 4.4 A textbook S90/Crossover pattern.
Courtesy of Concorde Forex Group, Inc.

MILLION-DOLLAR TIP

Multiple reasons to enter the market *decrease* your odds of a loss occurring. Hunches that the market will reverse for an entry *increase* your odds of a loss occurring.

Figure 4.1 shows the S90/Crossover strike at its best.

Figure 4.2 shows the S90/Crossover on the four-hour time compression, while Figure 4.3 shows the S90/Crossover on the two-hour time compression.

Finally, Figure 4.4 shows a textbook S90/Crossover pattern.

CHAPTER 5

S90/Crossover with Gaps, Holes, and Fibonacci Levels

The perfect S90/Crossover is found on a Fibonacci level when the horizontal line that is drawn from the original support or resistance of the founding trading range actually cuts precisely through a gap in the market. I am referring to the combination of a gap, Fib level, and an S90/Crossover.

This chapter provides 15 charts that illustrate these gaps; the captions on the figures explain the gaps, to help you understand the potential target values.

GAPS

Because the normal rule or thought about gaps is that they must be filled, the odds of filling the gap become extremely good, and you can see how many other types of confirmations will signal the return of the market to fill the gap. When an occurrence like this happens, you will observe that a perfectly precise S90/Crossover strike is often followed by an immediate reversal. If you're trading toward the gap, this type of target offers a second reversal entry with an extremely tight stop of normally less than 10 pips. As the market bounces from the strike, the reversal target should be a Fibonacci level based on the previous trading range, such as a .618, .50, or even .382 level.

Figure 5.1 illustrates a gap and how gaps are filled by bodies, not wicks.

HOLES IN THE MARKET

Patterns that appear on charts often have great significance; one of these patterns in particular is what I refer to as holes in the market. Figure 5.2 is an illustration of a hole

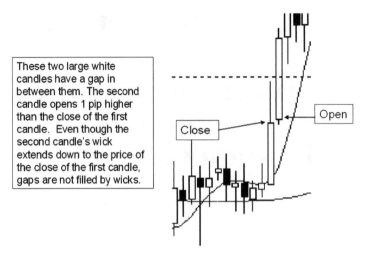

These two large white candles have a gap in between them. The second candle opens 1 pip higher than the close of the first candle. Even though the second candle's wick extends down to the price of the close of the first candle, gaps are not filled by wicks.

Close

Open

FIGURE 5.1 Illustration of a gap and how bodies, not wicks, fill gaps. Courtesy of Concorde Forex Group, Inc.

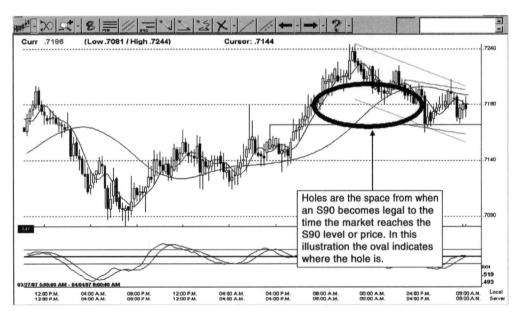

Holes are the space from when an S90 becomes legal to the time the market reaches the S90 level or price. In this illustration the oval indicates where the hole is.

FIGURE 5.2 Illustration of a hole in the market. Courtesy of Concorde Forex Group, Inc.

in the market—the space between when an S90 becomes legal and the time the market reaches the S90 level.

Figure 5.3 is an illustration of a large hole in the market, while Figure 5.4 is an illustration of a small hole in the market.

Figure 5.5 is another illustration of holes in the market.

Figure 5.6 shows how the perfect resistance crossover is found crossing over exactly at the bottom of the gap, and the perfect support crossover is found crossing over at the top of the gap. Another variable to consider regarding S90/Crossovers is what I call a first strike, shown in Figures 5.6 and 5.7. Figures 5.7 and 5.8 are found on 30-minute time compressions. Larger time compressions have more value and strength when the S90/Crossover is combined with a gap. Figure 5.9, a weekly chart, shows a gap that was filled in association with an S90/Crossover. Figure 5.10 illustrates another classic hole pattern.

There have been many books written about gaps. A gap is useful as long as it is a legal gap as opposed to an illegal gap. The difference is that an illegal gap appears due to data loss and the gap may not be filled at a later date, whereas a legitimate gap will be filled, especially if an S90/Crossover is involved.

Traders frequently do not consider the holes in the market that are often associated with the S90/Crossover. Small holes and larger holes all predict a return of the market

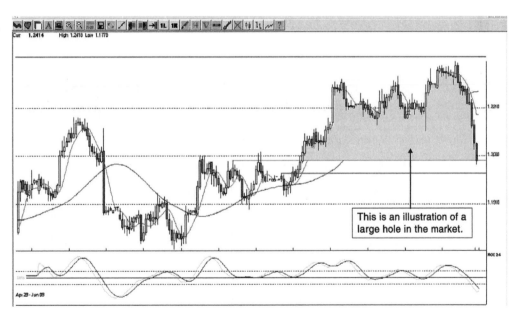

FIGURE 5.3 Illustration of a large hole in the market.
Courtesy of Concorde Forex Group, Inc.

FIGURE 5.4 Illustration of a small hole in the market.
Courtesy of Concorde Forex Group, Inc.

The first candle to open and close completely below the support line, which is the horizontal line, is a black candle with a long wick at the top. This candle turned the support into an S90. The very next candle is a small white candle. This white candle did not move up and touch the S90. The third candle, however, did, and then fell off. The distance between the top of the white candle and the S90 can be considered a hole. Holes can be generated with a single candle. General rule of thumb: The smaller the hole, the greater the subsequent move. You can see how much the market fell after the third candle touched the S90 for the first time after it became legal.

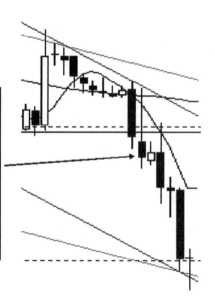

FIGURE 5.5 Illustration of a hole generated by a single candle.
Courtesy of Concorde Forex Group, Inc.

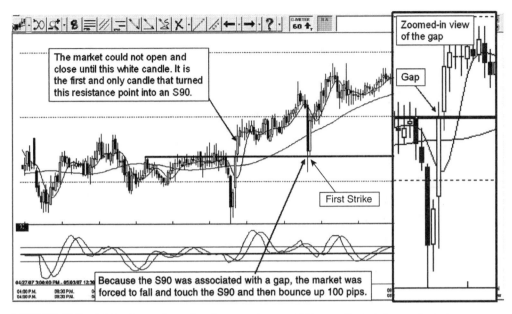

The market could not open and close until this white candle. It is the first and only candle that turned this resistance point into an S90.

Zoomed-in view of the gap

Gap

First Strike

Because the S90 was associated with a gap, the market was forced to fall and touch the S90 and then bounce up 100 pips.

FIGURE 5.6 A 30-minute chart showing a resistance S90, gap, first strike, and a hole. Courtesy of Concorde Forex Group, Inc.

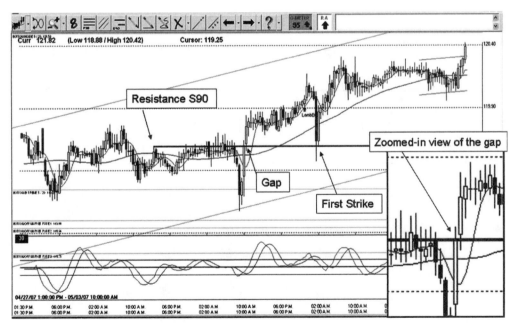

Resistance S90

Gap

First Strike

Zoomed-in view of the gap

FIGURE 5.7 A 30-minute chart showing a support S90, gap, first strike, and a hole. Courtesy of Concorde Forex Group, Inc.

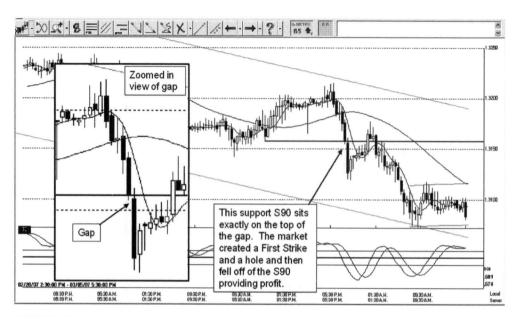

FIGURE 5.8 A perfect S90/Crossover with a horizontal line drawn through a gap with a first strike entry opportunity.
Courtesy of Concorde Forex Group, Inc.

FIGURE 5.9 Weekly chart illustration of a support S90, gap, first strike, and a hole.
Courtesy of Concorde Forex Group, Inc.

FIGURE 5.10 A classic hole pattern illustrating how holes play a part in S90s and the market.
Courtesy of Concorde Forex Group, Inc.

FIGURE 5.11 Five-minute chart showing that S90s and gaps can happen even on small time compressions.
Courtesy of Concorde Forex Group, Inc.

FIGURE 5.12 Zoomed-in view of the same five-minute S90 and gap as in Figure 5.11.
Courtesy of Concorde Forex Group, Inc.

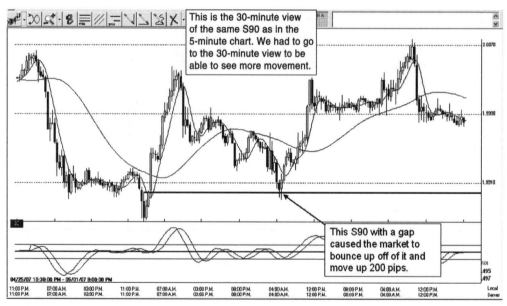

FIGURE 5.13 The 30-minute view of the same S90 as in Figures 5.11 and 5.12 shows subsequent
movement.
Courtesy of Concorde Forex Group, Inc.

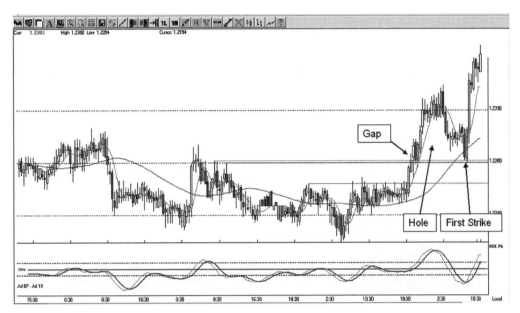

FIGURE 5.14 How resistance becomes support and how gaps, S90s, holes, and first strikes all play a role.
Courtesy of Concorde Forex Group, Inc.

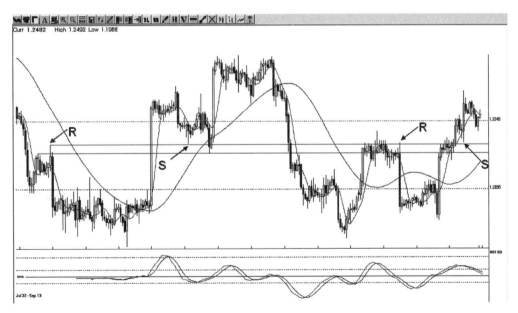

FIGURE 5.15 How resistance becomes support and vice versa.
Courtesy of Concorde Forex Group, Inc.

to certain historical areas, which will allow you to trade toward targets that fill holes. If by chance an S90/Crossover with a legal gap is in the target range of a market hole that needs to be filled, then the odds of the target being reached are very great.

In summary: When a hole is forming and an S90/Crossover and/or a gap that is close to the hole target become(s) apparent—and will be needed to complete the hole in the market—then the probability of a successful target strike has increased tremendously.

Smaller time compressions are not as reliable as larger compressions. In my opinion, starting with the 30-minute time frame and going higher toward the weekly time frame is much more valuable. I do know traders who trade in five-minute gaps and have been reasonably successful (as shown in Figures 5.11, 5.12, and 5.13), but their stops are usually greater than their profit targets; therefore, when a loss occurs, that loss usually takes all of the profits those traders have made from previous profitable gap entries.

Figures 5.14 and 5.15 show how resistance becomes support (and vice versa).

CHAPTER 6

Extreme Levels of a Trading Range

What Are S90/Crossover Extreme Levels within the Forex?

This seemingly simple question requires a rather complex answer. S90/Crossover extreme levels (ELs) are outer Fibonacci levels found within trading ranges that were former level one and two S90/Crossovers, which are also found within multiple time compressions of a trading range that have historical significance as overlapping Fibonacci points in the market. These levels are measured horizontally, vertically, diagonally, and with inverted reciprocal confirmations. Extreme levels have always been present, as have the laws of nature that Leonardo Fibonacci found in the early 1700s. The extreme levels represent expected support and resistance levels that are extensions from trading ranges that have historical significance. The extremes have outer layers of support and resistance that are seasonal, which are conclusive from studies that I have completed over the past few years. These extreme levels change as market conditions change on an almost daily basis.

If that sounds a bit confusing, don't worry. There is a simpler way to consider ELs. What really matters is that out of the millions of potential resistances, supports, or other levels that are present within trading ranges, you really just want to know which one will produce a sudden reversal or will best act as a target. You would at least expect to find an area of a newly developing trading range where a bend or reversal in the market may occur. If I were a beginning trader, I would say, "Don't tell me about it, just show me!" That's exactly what a charting package should offer: levels displayed and updated automatically each day to reveal potential targets and reversal entry points.

Here it is: Extremes appear, at this time, only on certain charts found within the industry. One of the companies that offer the extreme signals to the trading public has given permission to publish illustrations from the charts within this book. DGB

Technologies, LLC (which originally began as a sole proprietor company under another name and with no income) developed the charting software and white-labeled for resale the charts known as SmartCharts. DGB now has white-labeled the charting product to two forex companies: Concorde Forex Group, Inc. (CFG) (www.cfgtrading.com) and Forex Producers Group, LLC (FP) (www.forexproducers.com). Both of these companies offer the SmartCharts along with a free look before a subscription. I am sure there will be other companies offering the product soon. SmartCharts currently obtain data from almost 500 banks in order to feed a large amount of data into the charts in microsecond increments to create a real-time data feed experience. A massive amount of data is required to have an accurate reading for the extreme levels within the market. Other new charting services will most likely soon have the levels appearing on their chart applications as awareness of the accuracy of the extreme levels makes its way into the world of the forex.

To take advantage of this program, simply look at the charts each morning after the London open. The levels appear, automatically, between 3 A.M. and 7 A.M. eastern standard time (EST) on the charting service. If the market reaches these levels, then a possible entry may appear by most traditional technical systems, as well as with proprietary tools available on the market. Regardless of the type of alert system you're using, you must confirm and justify the signal before considering making an entry. Every entry must be confirmed.

For example, Figure 6.1 shows a five-minute time compression candlestick chart where the market strikes the upper extreme level twice before beginning its reversal. The upper extreme was posted approximately three hours before the strike occurred. The charts from this particular charting service, as illustrated in Figure 6.1, have horizontal lines that appear and refresh as updated trading ranges, which are projected about every 24 hours. Notice that the levels are labeled in Figure 6.1 as "top extreme" (in the upper left corner of the chart) and "top inside" (found at the lower left). If you move to a larger time compression (such as an hour chart or higher), then you can view the lower projected levels much more easily.

Figure 6.2 shows the $CAD (Canadian dollar) lower extreme: On May 5, 2005, the combination came within four pips of the lower level, which was 1.2425, for a bounce up and moved on up to 1.2470. The 1.2470, shown in Figure 6.2, allowed almost 50 pips of potential profit. The advance notice given to traders was about three hours. Extreme levels are considered by many to be an area in the market that will create a potential reversal. There are off-market levels that will bend the market as well, should the extreme levels become breached. There are reasons that extremes will be breached, and traders should trade the extreme levels with relatively tight stops of between 5 to 21 pips, based on whether a resistance or support appears in conjunction with the extreme level. I encourage this caution of placing a tight protective stop, just in case the level is not

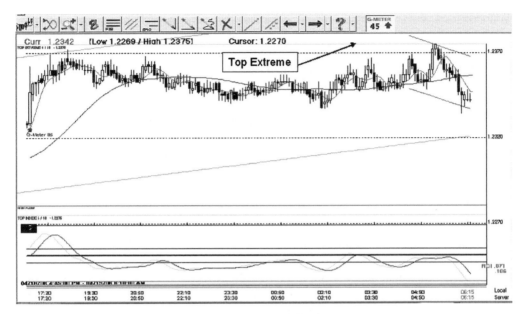

FIGURE 6.1 Five-minute chart showing top extreme level.
Courtesy of Concorde Forex Group, Inc.

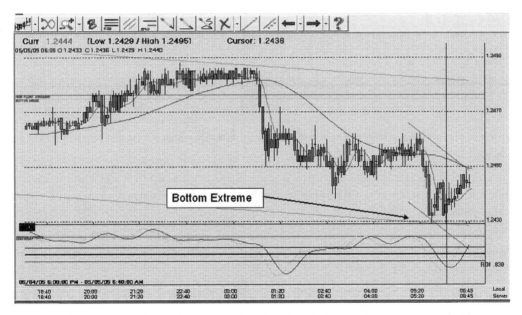

FIGURE 6.2 Five-minute chart of $CAD (Canadian dollar) showing bottom extreme level.
Courtesy of Concorde Forex Group, Inc.

honored for a reversal entry. The goal, obviously, is to minimize your risk and maximize your gain.

Figure 6.3 shows an Asian session where the British pound (GBP) was consolidating around the top inside wall. After the open of the London session, the GBP fell to the bottom inside wall. When the New York session opened later, the market breached the bottom inside and fell to the bottom extreme level of the trading range. This combination moved from the top inside wall to the bottom extreme level, providing a 200-pip move during a 24-hour period.

Figure 6.4 shows a strong S90/Crossover visible on the four-hour chart, down to the five-minute chart. In Figure 6.4, the S90/Crossover came down and landed exactly on top of the bottom inside wall. Having an extreme level or an inner channel wall overlap an S90/Crossover increases the odds for the market to return to that level. On this particular day, the market fell exactly to the S90/Crossover, which just happened to be a duplicate of the bottom inside wall for an extreme projection. This type of duplication is a great target to trade toward, and often additional confirmations are present for a reversal bounce trade entry, which may just add more pips to the margin. With the levels being hit exactly as displayed in this book (which also happens over and over again every month on all currency combinations), I believe this type of methodology has something to offer to every trader.

FIGURE 6.3 Illustration of a 200-pip move in the British pound through the Asian, London, and New York sessions.
Courtesy of Concorde Forex Group, Inc.

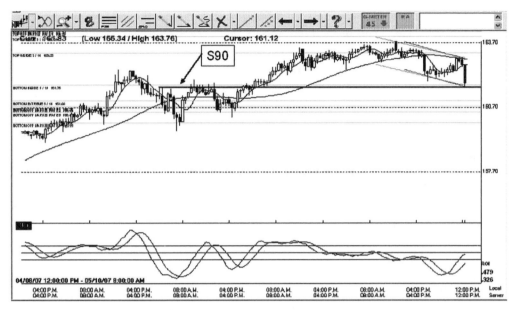

FIGURE 6.4 Illustration of a strong S90/Crossover.
Courtesy of Concorde Forex Group, Inc.

In previous sections of this book, S90Crossovers have been discussed, along with how they work with extreme levels. Although we have defined and explained the S90/Crossovers in previous chapters, let's review using a different approach. Let's ask the question again: What are these S90/Crossovers?

WHAT ARE S90/CROSSOVERS? THE COMPLEX ANSWER

S90/Crossovers are *originating supports* that occur on the *bottom* side of an *upward*-moving historical trading range and also as *originating resistances* on the *top* side of a *downward*-moving historical trading range. The supports and resistances have extensions and overlapping qualities that reveal the true Fibonacci levels that have more strength than others for possible profit targets and entries. There are four levels or tiers of the S90/Crossover to deal with, and most traders who learn the methodology are quite happy just to understand the first two tiers. The methodology (and it is a methodology) requires a thorough understanding of the legal and illegal aspects of the crossovers.

Level one S90/Crossovers are based upon support and resistance points that have legal and illegal qualifications to then become future targets as resistance points from former support levels and support points from former resistance levels.

Level two S90/Crossovers are associated with holes in the market where fresh S90/Crossovers have been birthed and the market comes back to strike the level as a possible reversal entry, leaving behind a hole the market.

Level three S90/Crossovers are associated with the extreme levels and inner walls, as well as the historical clusters associated with large and small trading ranges.

Level four S90/Crossovers deliver breakout points for possible entries from trend wall breaches and must be associated with larger compression ROI confirmations. (The rules of level four are confusing and may be misinterpreted easily without the guidance from a mentor especially when associated with the level three S90/Crossover.)

Again, there are four levels to the S90/Crossovers, and I've introduced only two levels of the system to the public. Before learning the last two levels, you must first master the first two levels. Training someone improperly will only cause confusion; therefore, it is important to have a certified mentor for training (as discussed in detail in Chapters 1 and 2). The last two levels remain as proprietary applications at this time and will be introduced to the world eventually.

WHAT ARE S90/CROSSOVERS? A SIMPLE ANSWER

The market has resistances and supports found within trading ranges and within the different time compressions. An S90/Crossover may appear on a 30-minute chart and not be recognized on a four-hour chart. Another example is that an S90/Crossover may appear on a five-minute compression but not be recognized on a 30-minute compression.

MILLION-DOLLAR TIP

The more time compressions that an S90/Crossover appears on at one time, especially if a legitimate gap is present, the better the odds that an entry into the market has been confirmed.

I recommend you reread the previous sentence to clearly understand this million-dollar tip.

Resistances often become supports in the future, as shown in Figure 6.5, and supports become resistances at a later time, as shown in Figures 6.6 and 6.7.

REQUIRED KNOWLEDGE AND TRAINING

Do you need to acquire any special knowledge or training before working with extreme levels?

FIGURE 6.5 Example of resistance becoming support.
Courtesy of Concorde Forex Group, Inc.

FIGURE 6.6 Example of support becoming resistance.
Courtesy of Concorde Forex Group, Inc.

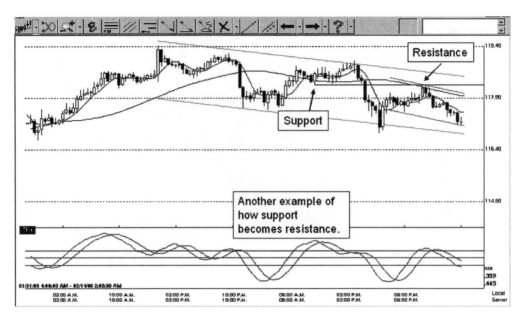

FIGURE 6.7 Example of support becoming resistance.
Courtesy of Concorde Forex Group, Inc.

Yes. Basic knowledge of trading methodology regarding trading ranges, resistance, support, trends, and how to enter market orders on a standard demo or live account is required for the execution of this type of trade entry. You should also know how to draw vertical and horizontal trend lines on the charts and be able to draw .382, .50, and .618 Fibonacci levels, which may correspond to the extreme levels or inner walls of a large trading range.

The tools needed to examine the trades should be SmartCharts (which you can obtain from both CFG and FP companies), which include signal indicators and River Channel Up/River Channel Down (RCU/RCD) extension clusters, as well as the calibrated river channel (RC) and River Oscillator Indicator (ROI) signal. You need these trading tools to be able to properly confirm the extreme indicators. The cost of these proprietary trading tools is insignificant, considering the possible profits that you can make as a result of the extreme and inner wall levels when associated with the S90/Crossovers.

CHAPTER 7

Basic Trading Skills with S90/Crossovers and Extreme Levels in the Market

L et's quickly review the basics of previous chapters to make sure you understand basic trading skills and their importance. After all, the S90/Crossovers are the foundation of the extreme levels in a trading range. You should have this general knowledge before proceeding; otherwise, you'll be confused as to how the markets work with the extreme levels of the forex.

TRADING RANGES

Trading ranges may be found between a resistance and a support on any time compression. Some traders may even consider trading ranges as small as a one-minute time compression if they are scalpers. Trading ranges have been considered as stabilized areas of the market; recently, however, more and more traders are beginning to realize that trading ranges shift as market conditions change. Extreme levels in the markets actually identify the larger ranges as they shift, and I have heard bank traders refer to the cause of these trading range shifts as "floating Fibonacci."

Traditionally, a range is identified as having lower lows and lower highs if in a bearish market or higher lows and higher highs if in a bull market. Trading ranges must be considered in all time compressions when trading, and to take advantage of the market, you need to open-mindedly understand the value of the S90/Crossovers as well as the extreme ranges in the markets.

RESISTANCE

The resistance becomes support at a later time, once a successful S90/Crossover has been identified. This is a million-dollar tip, especially if the level becomes a duplicated historical S90/Crossover.

SUPPORT

The support becomes resistance at a later time once a successful S90/Crossover has been identified.

TRENDS

The trend, when associated with a S90/Crossover, distinguishes between a false trend breakout and a true breakout. The *false* trend breakout allows a knowledgeable trader to enter a successful reversal, whereas the *true* breakout offers you safety regarding which direction to trade.

MARKET ORDERS

Market orders are those orders that traders enter based on a spontaneous decision to enter a trade. The decision could be based on a signal, a fundamental announcement, or even a hunch (which is most likely a mistake).

POSITION ORDERS

Position orders are usually based on a plan. These are used often for reversal entries well in advance of an S90/Crossover strike. Most traders plan a reversal entry if a gap, an S90/Crossover, and a Fibonacci level exist in the market that they can easily observe well in advance.

PLACING LIMITS

Most traders place limits to make sure profits are taken just before a target is reached. As the saying goes, a bird in the hand is worth two in the bush. This means if you are profiting and about to hit a level, the market may have to pass the strike point for you to obtain the desired exit.

Therefore, if you place your exit exactly on the target, you may suffer a reversal and reduced profits—if not a loss. Many traders do not use stops or understand the need to lock in profits before walking away from a computer. For example, if a perfect target is hit while you're asleep and the market reverses during the night, a great profit can turn into a great loss overnight. This is why it's so important to have a clear understanding of practicing placing limits and stops.

PLACING PROTECTIVE STOPS

According to every broker-dealer I have met, most traders do not place protective stops on their trades. They trade like gamblers trying to swing trade, with hopes that a trade gone bad will eventually come home for a profit. I have seen traders stay in a trade for days, creating stress while the trade is in the negative, until it comes back into profit and the trader exits proudly with two or three pips of profit. In my opinion, this is not good trading sense.

MILLION-DOLLAR TIP

Select a trade that has the greatest potential with the least amount of risk, and enter the trade with a profit target and an exit strategy.

TRAILING STOPS

A trailing stop offers a bit of protection to traders once the trade is showing profits; however, I have often found that when the market is really ready for a large move, the trailing stop is often taken out too early. In my opinion, the only acceptable way of chasing the market is the old-fashioned way: hands on. This hands-on approach is done by changing the stops to a position just below a newly formed support if the market is moving upward, and just above a newly formed resistance if the combination is bearish.

COST AVERAGING

There are several types or approaches to cost averaging a trade; the following paragraphs describe a couple of ways to consider this style of trading.

Cost Averaging Based on Directional Market Trends

I know traders who approach cost averaging by being convinced of the overall direction, based on larger time-compression signals as well as an overall view held by fundamentalists who state their direction views on financial programs or news segments on television as well as on the Internet with daily commentaries. Once the market direction is determined (i.e., whether it's bullish, bearish, or a lamb market), then these traders simply reenter in that direction at various levels as the market goes against the original entry point.

This style of trading quite often works if the trader has the financial ability to sustain a series of positions based on the size of the margin that is being traded and if there is a degree of stop tolerance rather than exhausting one's margin. Unfortunately, a lot of cost-averaging traders don't even use stops, and when they have losses, their losses are very large if they do not understand or have the self-discipline to cut their losses before draining their margin accounts.

On the positive side, if you have the ability to cost average and remain in the market with numerous cost-average entries, then your profit gains may be very impressive if traded back to the original or first entry made during the lengthy ordeal of this style of trading.

Cost Averaging Based on Mathematical or Fibonacci Levels

Another approach to cost averaging a trade is to consider using the logic of mathematical or Fibonacci levels based on previous trading ranges. If you're reasonably convinced of the market direction for the upcoming day or for the overall month, and if you measure the last levels of the previous trading ranges with Fibonacci ratios, then you can use these Fib levels as cost-average entry points.

If you have access to a charting service that has River Oscillator Indicator (ROI) channels and levels, the first cost-average entry will most likely be at the R3 or S3 level, depending on which way you're trading. If this level is breached, then the most logical area would be the R4 or S4 strike. If the R4 or S4 is breached, the R5 or S5 would be the third entry point. These levels of entry may continue on to the six or seven strongest areas of resistance and supports or until a stop tolerance has been reached.

I have always told traders that if you are not 99 percent positive of the market direction, you can always cut your losses early on a bad trade. You can get back in the trade later without risking multiple-entry losses. One observation I have made over the years is that if a trade seems to go bad for smaller margin traders after they had identified the overall direction, they were usually right in their original assessment. As soon as the exit is made, the market turns and would have paid the small trader a profit.

Traders with sustaining power then take all the profits and brag about what good traders they are.

To overcome exiting too early, and if you just don't have a lot of money in the margin, then deal with what you have and exit smartly early on; wait for the combination to get where it's going against all the cost-averaging traders and losers in the market; then reenter, because there seems to always be a new entry signal around R3 or S3 and those levels beyond. Once you've entered, then you should ride the trade all the way back to the original entry that you had exited and not only capture back your funds lost, but capture new profits as well.

Summary of Cost-Averaging Procedures

As mentioned earlier, there are several procedures involved in the skill of cost averaging in the marketplace. In summary: The basic cost-averaging procedure that a larger precentage of traders use is to reenter the market as it goes against your trade a few or numerous times at specific predetermined levels, which are usually based on Fibonacci levels, until the trade eventually returns to the original target.

If you have substantial sustaining power by having a very large margin in your trading account, you can profit by using applied cost- averaging procedures and not the original trade entry. As you take profits from multiple entries, by the time the original target is reached, you will usually escape the trade with a pip or so per lot on the original trade, while taking the most profits from your cost-average entries.

Therefore, to reiterate: The real trade was not the original trade; instead, it was the multiple entries from the cost averaging.

This cost-averaging style of trading is often referred to as one of the three methods of trading against the crowd. For example, in a bull market, the overall industry is trading up, and you are also trading up; however, as the market begins to fall against the crowd, you continue with additional entries up. You are hoping that, as other traders get knocked out of the market with their stops or small sustaining abilities, you, the cost-averaging trader, will mop up (so to speak) with multiple entries up.

EFFECTS OF OVERLAPPING FIBONACCI LEVELS

As trading ranges are formed, Fibonacci levels may be measured. The center level is .50 or 50 percent from the top high to the low of a range made up of bull and bear candlesticks. The other two important levels that most traders focus on are the .382 and .618 levels.

Imagine the human body as having the following assigned levels: the chest at .382, the waist at .50, and the knees at .618.

A trading range works the same way, All-time lows and highs or new highs and lows that go beyond former highs and lows are considered 1.27s, as markets reach beyond the head and feet areas.

When an S90/Crossover appears to rest on top of a trading range Fib level, you will see a stall or bounce in the market as a strike is made. If a gap is involved, then this becomes a very strong target to trade toward and also a possible reversal entry point.

Merging S90/Crossovers and extreme levels (ELs) in the market offers you a more precise entry, as long as confirmations are present to justify an entry if you are expecting a reversal as the market approaches the EL.

If you are trading toward the EL and an S90/Crossover is in the general area, then the level also becomes a target to trade toward.

Because projected trading ranges shift almost daily at times, new support- or resistant-based S90/Crossovers often appear as a shift in the daily projected range opens new opportunities for targets and entries.

If an upper extreme remains the same as the market moves in the opposite direction, it means that if there is a gap associated with the S90/Crossover, then the market often will eventually move toward the level as a strong target.

CHAPTER 8

S90/Crossovers, Trend Bounces, and Holes in the Market

I t is my belief that just about anyone, with time and practice, can develop peripheral awareness in the market. Observing uptrends and downtrends that may be viewed within larger time compressions as trends will reveal S90/Crossovers, just as vertical trading ranges will. The illustrations in this chapter offer a few different views of how Fibonacci levels may be observed, as well as trading ranges or trends within trends.

Figure 8.1 is a view of trends within trends. This main trend is an uptrend. Within this, there are smaller downtrends. Trends within trends can happen on any time compression and any chart: The market has to go down to go up and vice versa.

A weekly candlestick chart has 2,016 five-minute candles that have been moving in uptrend and downtrend patterns for a week before a weekly candle has had time to mature. Let's assume that white candles are bullish and dark candles are bearish:

- On a five-minute time compression, if the bulls were in power during a week, then more white candles will be present, and the one weekly candle that will appear at the end of the week as a summary of the historical trading that has been completed for the week will be a white candle, representing that there were more buyers in the market than sellers during the previous week.
- If more dark candles are present on the five-minute chart than white candles during a given week, then bears were in control, and the one weekly candle that will appear at the end of the week as a summary of the historical trading that has been completed for the week will be a dark candle.

A one-hour candlestick represents the price action of 12 five-minute candles; the 30-minute candle is the equivalent of 6 five-minute candles; and the four-hour candle

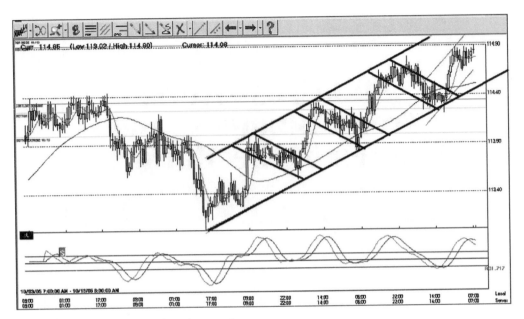

FIGURE 8.1 View of trends within trends.
Courtesy of Concorde Forex Group, Inc.

comprises 48 five-minute candles; and so on with any time compression. There is a lot going on within each time compression, and any time something or a pattern is being duplicated, you should become aware of potential or possibilities of profitable trading entries or exits, especially if you're already in a trade.

We should look at trends, Fibonacci levels, and S90/Crossovers that may be found in all time compressions in regard to their particular world. A five-minute world is much different than one found within a one-hour chart compression or a daily chart. Most traders focus on drawing horizontal lines based on derived levels from a vertical view of their favorite time compressions. In contrast, more advanced traders not only consider several time compressions but also draw uphill and downhill lines to follow the trends as they look for breakouts to enter. Along with the trend wall breach entries, traders may look for gaps, S90/Crossovers, and/or ROI Fibonacci strikes as possible targets or entries. This type of peripheral awareness in the market, which allows you, as a trader, to turn over all of the stones, develops with time and eventually becomes automatic—just like driving a car, flying an airplane, or riding a bicycle. Traders eventually become automated at recognizing opportunities and confirmations for a trade. It just takes patience, time, practice—and sometimes a lot of money if you're not selective.

Assuming we are working with a downtrend, you would use a slow- and-fast-moving volume average, and begin by drawing the trend line for the resistance side of the trend, as illustrated in Figure 8.2. Once you've drawn that trend line, then you can begin looking

FIGURE 8.2 Example of drawing trend lines.
Courtesy of Concorde Forex Group, Inc.

at other types of confirmations. (Traditional confirmations are not explored in this book, because the focus in on modernism and proprietary systems.)

Notice that the line is drawn down and connected at the top of the resistance points. When the market breaks through the level as a reversal, the market offers an entry point at the breaching point—provided other volume indicators (such as an ROI) are in agreement. If the market does not come back and open and close below the trend line after the reversal, then it is considered a legal crossover. In the future, if the market comes back to this level, it should bounce off the level as a possible new reversal entry—especially if there is also a horizontal S90/Crossover and/or a Fib level in the general area of the S90/Crossover trend wall strike. This sounds very complicated, but Figure 8.3 should help you grasp the concept.

Figure 8.3 demonstrates the return of the market and a bounce trade opportunity. Notice the hole or space that was created during the market each time it returned to the trend line. This hole is something that many traders do not count as a confirmation for a future trade; however, a second deliberate hole in the market with volume indicators in agreement regarding direction of the market flow has generated many positive trades for those who have open minds to learning something different.

Figure 8.4 recognizes a second hole that has developed from a trend wall that will eventually offer a trend wall S90/Crossover. The market breached the trend wall after forming a second hole in the market. The breach was justified by the trend wall and

FIGURE 8.3 Example of the market returning to the trend line.
Courtesy of Concorde Forex Group, Inc.

FIGURE 8.4 Example of a market breaching the trend wall after forming a second hole.
Courtesy of Concorde Forex Group, Inc.

additional confirmations that were related to volume indicators. Larger time compressions are best suited for this trade entry.

Here's what Figure 8.5 shows us (note this is the same chart as Figure 8.2):

- Point A to point B is hole #1 for the uptrend.
- Point B to point D is hole #2 for the uptrend.
- When the market created point D, the oscillating indicator at the bottom of the chart was heading down. This means that the market was more likely to fall than to rise. This is what we refer to as a breach: The market could not stay above of the trend line.
- The majority of the time after a breach, the market will hook back to the trend line and then continue the move away. This hook is represented by point E.

In the case of an uptrend, a trend line is drawn by connecting the bottom supports. Figure 8.5 shows the return of the market and a bounce trade opportunity as a result of an uptrend, with the market coming to a trend line and having some sort of reaction as either a bounce or a breach. The prediction of direction is usually detected by smaller time compression ROIs. Just as in the previous example in Figure 8.4 of a downtrend, notice the hole or space that was created during the market return in this example.

FIGURE 8.5 Example of a market breaching the trend wall after forming a second hole. Courtesy of Concorde Forex Group, Inc.

As mentioned earlier, a hole or semicircle found within the trend is something that many traders do not count as a confirmation for a future trade; however, a second deliberate hole in the market with volume indicators in agreement regarding direction of the market flow has continued to generate many positive trades. Although all time compressions may offer this type of entry opportunity, larger time compressions are best suited for a trade entry of this type due to the recognition of more volume. As with any trade, the more volume, the more opportunity will be present as well as risk.

In the previous example, I talked about holes of an uptrend. Points AB is hole #1, and points BD represent hole #2. Point D is the breach to signal a downward move. Point E shows how the market can hook back up to the trend line and bounce off of it to continue the downtrend. Because we now have a downtrend, point C comes into play. Point E is the hook for the uptrend, but it doubles as a point of resistance for holes of a downtrend. Points CE is hole #1 in the downtrend, and points EF is hole #2. At the time point F was created, the oscillating indicator at the bottom of the chart was headed up, meaning the market had more of a chance to climb rather than fall.

What I refer to as "holes in the market" may sometimes confuse traders because they think of a complete circle, but I am referring to a half circle. A 30-minute half circle is found to be different from a 10-minute, two-hour, and one-day chart half circle or for any time compression. A five-minute hole may not be recognized by larger time compressions, similar to the way a five-minute resistance is not recognized by larger time compressions. A four-hour hole may not be noticed or duplicated in the weekly chart, because they represent (to me) different time compression worlds. A trader may find that the same visual feature, pattern, or signal is not found in multiple time compressions on almost all signals. However, if a signal is found in multiple time compressions, then this becomes a very strong level or signal to either enter the market or exit if you are approaching one of these representations.

A simple example of this is a resistance point. As defined, a resistance point is a high with two lower candles to the left and right of the resistance top. A five-minute candle may offer a perfect resistance point, but then if you go to the four-hour chart, most of the time you will not find that perfect high, because it is buried within a single four-hour candle that is made up of 48 five-minute candles. It is the same with the holes in the market: A 30-minute hole may not be viewed in all instances on larger time compressions. Therefore, if you do find a match on all time compressions, then a possible reversal is often imminent—and even this great duplicated combination of signals needs additional confirmations to increase your safety in the market.

CHAPTER 9

Proof: Live Forex Trading Examples and Interviews with Traders

I s there existing proof that this type of trading application actually works? Yes! The proof is in the form of live trading histories provided by traders who are associated with Concorde Forex Group, Inc. (CFG), also known as CFGTrading (www.cfgtrading.com). Other companies that hold proven copies of trading histories are Forex Producers Group, LLC (www.forexproducers.com) and the Independent Forex Traders Association (www.IFxTA.com). Copies of live trading histories have been provided to these companies voluntarily by associated traders from around the world who are involved with these organizations. The trading histories are found at CFGTrading headquarters and at the Independent Forex Traders Association. Both organizations are located in Richmond, Virginia. There are also samples of these trading histories located at the home office of the Forex Producers Group, LLC, located in Jacksonville, Florida. Traders around the world have come to visit the headquarters of the Concorde Forex Group company for tours of the facilities as well as to view the many thick books of live trading history archives that are available for inspection.

The newest organization among the three companies is Forex Producers Group, LLC, which emerged during 2006 to bring this unique trading style up to the advanced level by the use of automated software with a testing vehicle to move traders to each skill level of trading. The web site (www.forexproducers.com) demands proof from traders of previous successful trading performance before entry is even allowed into the vault of success. This company means business and is intended exclusively for the serious student of the forex.

The live trading histories provided in this chapter are intentionally small so as not to lead traders to believe that earning $20,000 or $100,000 per week is easy (although it is possible). Although large amounts are earned in the market every day, when trading on the forex you should start from the bottom and work your way to the top, just as you would with any job. You can visit one of the companies previously mentioned and view live trading histories that show earnings exceeding $100,000 per week, with string trading histories exceeding 200 trades in a row.*

The S90/Crossover with extreme levels does not guarantee anyone success, because not everyone will execute the trades the same way due to individual interpretations of signals. This is probably because some individuals simply will not follow the procedural instructions, which require tight stops placed as well as outer-level entry executions discussed later in Chapter 10. Misinterpretation is one possible route to failure, as is what I call a lack of market emotional stability.

For you (or anyone) to be successful with any methodology, it is necessary to develop maturity in the market. This requires time, patience, and ongoing study. There is no instant success in the markets, and you have to pay your dues on demo and small live accounts. Begin practicing the extreme levels on a demo; then try the procedures on a live mini account to test the waters. If you are successful with a live mini account, then you can consider a live standard account. Easing into the markets with a new trading concept after you develop the proper skills allows time for you to build confidence in your ability. Taking a slower and selective type of approach to learning how to trade the forex allows you to overcome the greatest obstacle, which is found between your ears! In the end, success is all about your emotion in the market and how you react or respond to it.

I suggest that a beginner be very realistic and trade at least 50 trades in a row on a demo without a loss while using a protective stop before going live. The purpose of trading a minimum of 50 trades in a row without a loss on a demo account is to prove to yourself that you have the self discipline to be a selective and cautious trader before trading on a live account. It only makes sense to use the same amount in the practice account that will be used when eventually going live. Once you open a live mini account, use the same caution and selective entry approach that you used in your demo account. It is a simple fact that if you cannot become successful with a demo and a live mini account, the odds are you will not succeed by investing a large amount into a standard account.

---

*__Disclaimer__: Trading the foreign exchange market carries a high level of risk and may not be suitable for all investors. Before deciding to trade the foreign exchange market, you should carefully consider your investment objectives, level of experience, and risk appetite. The possibility exists that you could sustain a loss of some or all of your initial investment; therefore, you should not invest money that you cannot afford to lose. You should be aware of all the risk associated with foreign currency exchange trading, and you should seek advice from an independent financial advisor if you have any doubts.

The following two examples of live trading histories illustrate the potential earnings of a trader in the forex. Beginner-type trading histories are illustrated only, and I am sure that many intermediate or seasoned traders could have this type of consecutive trading success.

Only smaller live trading accounts are illustrated in this book; if you're interested in viewing larger production numbers, please contact me at Don@SelectiveForex Trading.com. Taken alone, these illustrations should not sway you to begin trading the forex. Everyone will perform differently in the trading industry, and this is not a "pie in the sky" business. The currency trading industry may sometimes be a very serious and dangerous business. Ease into the business gradually to determine whether you are suited to become a professional full-time or part-time trader.

EXAMPLE #1: LIVE TRADING HISTORY BY A NEOPHYTE TRADER

The example shown in Figure 9.1 is of a live trading account. Here are the facts:

- The starting live date was March 1, 2006, and the ending date for the 50+ trades was April 4, 2006.
- The total gross profit was $4,429.40.
- The start-up margin was $5,000 (U.S. dollars) on a standard account.
- The margin basis was a 200:1 ratio, or $500, as required per lot to trade.

Figure 9.1 has a couple of negatives on the net profit/loss (P/L), which were caused by staying in a trade a little too long, thus causing interest to be charged for the overnight stay. However, if you look at the gross P/L, you will observe more than 50 trades in a row without a negative.

These examples of live trading histories are for illustration and study purposes only.

Interview with Anonymous Trader #1

"This was the first time that I traded live. I completed 50 trades in a row on a demo before going live; still, I found trading was a lot different when I was trading live.

"I did have a couple of negatives on the net profit column. These happened because I entered the trade and had to stay in the trade for a long time. The interest charged kept eating up my profits until I could get out. When the market finally showed a profit on my dealing station, I forgot to look at the expenses of the overnight trade and clicked out with a profit. I should have stayed in the trade longer to cover the charges, but my gross did show profit."

Trade Account Number: XXXXXXXX Created at: Oct 4, 2001 11:10:33 AM Status: Active

CLOSED TRADE LIST

Ticket #	Currency	Volume	Date	Sold	Bought	Gross P/L	Comm	Inter	Adj	Net P/L	Condition	Created by
33305	EUR/USD	100K	03/01/06 01:07 PM	1.1905							Mkt	
			03/07/06 06:56 AM		1.1900	**50.00**	0.00	−45.30	0.00	4.70	L	
33354	AUD/USD	100K	03/01/06 01:19 PM	0.7443							Mkt	
			03/03/06 10:03 AM		0.7439	**40.00**	0.00	−8.60	0.00	31.40	C	
38526	EUR/USD	100K	03/02/06 02:25 PM	1.2034							LE	
			03/02/06 08:07 PM		1.2022	**120.00**	0.00	−7.55	0.00	112.45	C	
41869	USD/CHF	100K	03/03/06 09:13 AM	1.2977							Mkt	
			03/03/06 10:02 AM	1.2982		**38.51**	0.00	0.00	0.00	38.51	L	
41905	USD/CAD	100K	03/03/06 09:22 AM	1.1331							Mkt	
			03/03/06 10:12 AM	1.1353		**193.78**	0.00	0.00	0.00	193.78	C	
41959	EUR/USD	100K	03/03/06 09:30 AM	1.2047							Mkt	
			03/03/06 10:06 AM		1.2011	**360.00**	0.00	0.00	0.00	360.00	L	
43291	GBP/USD	100K	03/03/06 11:06 AM	1.7531							Mkt	
			03/03/06 11:31 AM		1.7520	**110.00**	0.00	0.00	0.00	110.00	L	
45233	EUR/USD	100K	03/05/06 07:26 PM	1.2072							Mkt	
			03/06/06 03:58 AM		1.2052	**200.00**	0.00	0.00	0.00	200.00	L	
51902	EUR/USD	100K	03/07/06 07:32 AM	1.1910							Mkt	
			03/07/06 07:40 AM		1.1915	**50.00**	0.00	0.00	0.00	50.00	L	
52024	USD/CAD	100K	03/07/06 08:13 AM	1.1449							Mkt	
			03/07/06 08:21 AM		1.1444	**43.69**	0.00	0.00	0.00	43.69	L	
56781	USD/CAD	100K	03/08/06 10:05 AM	1.1533							Mkt	
			03/08/06 10:31 AM		1.1530	**26.02**	0.00	0.00	0.00	26.02	C	
57233	USD/CAD	100K	03/08/06 11:40 AM	1.1559							Mkt	
			03/08/06 05:42 PM		1.1556	**25.96**	0.00	−8.70	0.00	17.26	C	
57274	USD/CAD	100K	03/08/06 11:53 AM	1.1575							Mkt	
			03/08/06 05:42 PM		1.1556	**164.42**	0.00	−8.70	0.00	155.72	C	
57508	EUR/USD	100K	03/08/06 01:04 PM	1.1931							Mkt	
			03/08/06 07:36 PM		1.1933	**20.00**	0.00	−22.65	0.00	−2.65	C	
57526	USD/CHF	100K	03/08/06 01:10 PM	1.3075							Mkt	
			03/08/06 07:36 PM		1.3070	**38.26**	0.00	−31.05	0.00	7.21	C	
60110	USD/CHF	100K	03/09/06 05:26 AM	1.3094							Mkt	
			03/09/06 05:35 AM		1.3089	**38.20**	0.00	0.00	0.00	38.20	C	
64410	EUR/USD	100K	03/10/06 04:20 AM	1.1923							Mkt	
			03/10/06 04:32 AM		1.1922	**10.00**	0.00	0.00	0.00	10.00	C	
67227	GBP/USD	100K	03/10/06 09:19 AM	1.7271							Mkt	
			03/10/06 09:23 AM		1.7264	**70.00**	0.00	0.00	0.00	70.00	C	
67388	GBP/USD	100K	03/10/06 09:24 AM	1.7248							Mkt	
			03/10/06 10:20 AM		1.7247	**10.00**	0.00	0.00	0.00	10.00	L	
67497	EUR/USD	100K	03/10/06 09:30 AM	1.1870							Mkt	
			03/10/06 09:37 AM		1.1865	**50.00**	0.00	0.00	0.00	50.00	C	
67870	USD/CAD	100K	03/10/06 09:56 AM	1.1634							Mkt	
			03/10/06 10:22 AM		1.1631	**25.79**	0.00	0.00	0.00	25.79	C	
73976	GBP/USD	100K	03/13/06 11:31 AM	1.7318							Mkt	
			03/13/06 12:21 PM		1.7301	**170.00**	0.00	0.00	0.00	170.00	C	
74021	EUR/USD	100K	03/13/06 11:43 AM	1.1940							Mkt	
			03/13/06 12:54 PM		1.1937	**30.00**	0.00	0.00	0.00	30.00	C	
75624	EUR/USD	100K	03/13/06 08:10 PM	1.1967							Mkt	
			03/13/06 08:16 PM		1.1962	**50.00**	0.00	0.00	0.00	50.00	C	
78288	EUR/USD	100K	03/14/06 09:58 AM	1.1984							Mkt	
			03/23/06 10:29 AM		1.1978	**60.00**	0.00	−73.70	0.00	−13.70	L	

FIGURE 9.1 Live Trading History by a Neophyte Trader, 50+ Trades

80061 EUR/USD 100K	03/14/06 04:52 PM 1.2010								Mkt	
	03/23/06 10:28 AM	1.1988	**220.00**	0.00	−73.70	0.00	146.30	C	
84256 AUD/USD 100K	03/15/06 12:21 PM 0.7380								Mkt	
	03/15/06 11:49 PM	0.7374	**60.00**	0.00	−6.00	0.00	54.00	L	
84408 GBP/USD 100K	03/15/06 01:26 PM 1.7462								Mkt	
	03/15/06 11:46 PM	1.7457	**50.00**	0.00	−3.30	0.00	46.70	L	
96712 EUR/USD 100K	03/19/06 09:20 PM 1.2174								Mkt	
	03/20/06 09:51 AM	1.2163	**110.00**	0.00	0.00	0.00	110.00	C	
99549 EUR/JPY 100K	03/20/06 12:21 PM 141.49								Mkt	
	03/20/06 04:54 PM 141.59		**85.93**	0.00	0.00	0.00	85.93	L	
00554 NZD/USD 100K	03/20/06 07:30 PM	0.6238							Mkt	
	03/20/06 07:44 PM 0.6245		**70.00**	0.00	0.00	0.00	70.00	L	
02591 EUR/USD 100K	03/21/06 08:26 AM 1.2150								Mkt	
	03/21/06 08:58 AM	1.2139	**110.00**	0.00	0.00	0.00	110.00	C	
04095 EUR/USD 100K	03/21/06 10:51 AM 1.2090								Mkt	
	03/21/06 10:54 AM	1.2088	**20.00**	0.00	0.00	0.00	20.00	L	
06771 GBP/USD 100K	03/22/06 04:11 AM	1.7491							Mkt	
	03/22/06 09:27 AM 1.7492		**10.00**	0.00	0.00	0.00	10.00	L	
07364 GBP/JPY 100K	03/22/06 08:00 AM 204.33								Mkt	
	03/22/06 08:31 AM	204.15	**154.08**	0.00	0.00	0.00	154.08	L	
08026 USD/JPY 100K	03/22/06 10:00 AM 116.82								Mkt	
	03/22/06 10:18 AM	116.72	**85.68**	0.00	0.00	0.00	85.68	L	
08034 GBP/JPY 100K	03/22/06 10:03 AM 204.27								Mkt	
	03/22/06 10:23 AM	204.05	**188.65**	0.00	0.00	0.00	188.65	L	
09612 EUR/JPY 100K	03/22/06 07:31 PM 141.15								Mkt	
	03/22/06 07:53 PM	141.07	**68.45**	0.00	0.00	0.00	68.45	L	
09749 USD/JPY 100K	03/22/06 08:04 PM 116.82								Mkt	
	03/22/06 08:17 PM	116.77	**42.82**	0.00	0.00	0.00	42.82	C	
09834 EUR/USD 100K	03/22/06 08:19 PM 1.2055								Mkt	
	03/23/06 10:02 AM	1.2040	**150.00**	0.00	0.00	0.00	150.00	L	
13706 AUD/USD 100K	03/23/06 01:24 PM 0.7145								Mkt	
	03/23/06 03:14 PM	0.7144	**10.00**	0.00	0.00	0.00	10.00	L	
14614 USD/JPY 100K	03/23/06 06:41 PM 117.80								Mkt	
	03/24/06 10:16 AM	117.79	**8.49**	0.00	0.00	0.00	8.49	L	
25677 GBP/USD 100K	03/28/06 06:31 AM 1.7476								Mkt	
	03/28/06 02:21 PM	1.7470	**60.00**	0.00	0.00	0.00	60.00	L	
26724 EUR/USD 100K	03/28/06 10:05 AM 1.2078								Mkt	
	03/28/06 10:44 AM	1.2073	**50.00**	0.00	0.00	0.00	50.00	C	
31859 USD/JPY 200K	03/29/06 04:09 AM	117.95							Mkt	
	03/29/06 06:25 AM 118.02		**118.62**	0.00	0.00	0.00	118.62	L	
32003 USD/CAD 100K	03/29/06 05:12 AM 1.1727								Mkt	
	03/29/06 08:28 AM	1.1715	**102.43**	0.00	0.00	0.00	102.43	C	
32451 USD/CAD 100K	03/29/06 07:37 AM 1.1727								Mkt	
	03/29/06 08:28 AM	1.1715	**102.43**	0.00	0.00	0.00	102.43	C	
32661 GBP/USD 200K	03/29/06 08:41 AM	1.7355							Mkt	
	03/29/06 11:41 AM 1.7361		**120.00**	0.00	0.00	0.00	120.00	C	
32970 GBP/USD 200K	03/29/06 09:40 AM	1.7341							Mkt	
	03/29/06 11:32 AM 1.7353		**240.00**	0.00	0.00	0.00	240.00	C	
36402 EUR/USD 200K	03/30/06 06:21 AM	1.2080							Mkt	
	03/30/06 06:32 AM 1.2082		**40.00**	0.00	0.00	0.00	40.00	C	
44529 GBP/USD 200K	03/31/06 10:03 AM 1.7337								Mkt	
	04/02/06 11:02 PM	1.7330	**140.00**	0.00	−4.20	0.00	135.80	L	
56856 USD/CAD 200K	04/04/06 01:08 PM	1.1637							LE	
	04/04/06 07:36 PM 1.1638		**17.19**	0.00	−6.10	0.00	11.09	C	
Total:			**4,429.40**	0.00	−299.55	0.00	4,129.85		
Posted at statement period of time:			**4,429.40**	0.00	−270.45	0.00			

FIGURE 9.1 *(Continued)*

What You Can Learn from This Example

Beginning traders should not skip the time necessary to pay the dues of practicing on a demo even after going live. To reiterate, it is just senseless to begin trading live before proving to yourself that you can actually trade with discipline. Even then, you shouldn't place a lot of money into a margin because it is a totally different experience once you begin live trading. After going live, I recommend you enter the market with a small amount of live margin funds on a mini live account to begin testing your emotions and your discipline (which you should have developed on the demo). I am sure most people have heard that it's better to get your toes wet and ease in than to just jump in and start swimming; it's the same with the market.

EXAMPLE #2: LIVE BEGINNING TRADER, 90+ TRADES IN A ROW WITHOUT A LOSS

Figure 9.2 shows the results of another actual live trading account history, taken from a small margin account containing only $2,000 of margin at the beginning of March 2006 and ending with $10,620.16 on April 21, 2006. This type of success does not imply that everyone will have the same success, and you should take time to read the disclaimers throughout the book. *There are no guarantees in the market, and there are no guarantees in life.* Once a driver has a license, we all know that everyone will drive a car differently, and some will crash on the road. This applies to the market and a margin account as well: Crashes occur every day in the market, and selective trading combined with commonsense applications increases the odds for success.

Notice the transactions include all of the following information:

- The ticket number for trade identification.
- The combination (currency) traded.
- The volume.
- The date of the entry and exit.
- The levels of entry and exit.
- The gross profit/loss.

Figure 9.2 should give beginning traders an idea of what to expect, as success gradually develops for this beginning trader. This example illustrates a $10,620.16 profit in less than two months while trading on a standard account. As mentioned, the beginning balance for the margin was $2,000.

Interview with Anonymous Trader #2

"I attended formal training before opening and trading a live account. I attended a two-day training session and paid a mentor to explain the language of a proprietary

Statement Period: from Mar 1, 2006 5:00:00 PM through Apr 21, 2006 4:31:00 PM

User Name: XXXXXXXXX

Trade Account Number: 0000XXXX: Status: Active

CLOSED TRADE LIST

Ticket #	Currency	Volume	Date	Sold	Bought	Gross P/L
503	EUR/USD	100K	03/01/06 01:07 PM	1.1905		
			03/07/06 06:56 AM		1.1900	**50.00**
503	AUD/USD	100K	03/01/06 01:19 PM	0.7443		
			03/03/06 10:03 AM		0.7439	**40.00**
503	EUR/USD	100K	03/02/06 02:25 PM	1.2034		
			03/02/06 08:07 PM		1.2022	**120.00**
504	USD/CHF	100K	03/03/06 09:13 AM		1.2977	
			03/03/06 10:02 AM	1.2982		**38.51**
905	USD/CAD	100K	03/03/06 09:22 AM		1.1331	
			03/03/06 10:12 AM	1.1353		**193.78**
959	EUR/USD	100K	03/03/06 09:30 AM	1.2047		
			03/03/06 10:06 AM		1.2011	**360.00**
291	GBP/USD	100K	03/03/06 11:06 AM	1.7531		
			03/03/06 11:31 AM		1.7520	**110.00**
233	EUR/USD	100K	03/05/06 07:26 PM	1.2072		
			03/06/06 03:58 AM		1.2052	**200.00**
902	EUR/USD	100K	03/07/06 07:32 AM		1.1910	
			03/07/06 07:40 AM	1.1915		**50.00**
024	USD/CAD	100K	03/07/06 08:13 AM	1.1449		
			03/07/06 08:21 AM		1.1444	**43.69**
781	USD/CAD	100K	03/08/06 10:05 AM	1.1533		
			03/08/06 10:31 AM		1.1530	**26.02**
233	USD/CAD	100K	03/08/06 11:40 AM	1.1559		
			03/08/06 05:42 PM		1.1556	**25.96**
274	USD/CAD	100K	03/08/06 11:53 AM	1.1575		
			03/08/06 05:42 PM		1.1556	**164.42**
508	EUR/USD	100K	03/08/06 01:04 PM		1.1931	
			03/08/06 07:36 PM	1.1933		**20.00**
526	USD/CHF	100K	03/08/06 01:10 PM	1.3075		
			03/08/06 07:36 PM		1.3070	**38.26**
110	USD/CHF	100K	03/09/06 05:26 AM	1.3094		
			03/09/06 05:35 AM		1.3089	**38.20**
410	EUR/USD	100K	03/10/06 04:20 AM	1.1923		
			03/10/06 04:32 AM		1.1922	**10.00**

(Continues)

FIGURE 9.2 Live Trading History by a Beginning Trader, 90+ Trades in a Row

Ticket #	Currency	Volume	Date	Sold	Bought	Gross P/L
227	GBP/USD	100K	03/10/06 09:19 AM	1.7271		
			03/10/06 09:23 AM		1.7264	**70.00**
388	GBP/USD	100K	03/10/06 09:24 AM	1.7248		
			03/10/06 10:20 AM		1.7247	**10.00**
497	EUR/USD	100K	03/10/06 09:30 AM	1.1870		
			03/10/06 09:37 AM		1.1865	**50.00**
870	USD/CAD	100K	03/10/06 09:56 AM	1.1634		
			03/10/06 10:22 AM		1.1631	**25.79**
976	GBP/USD	100K	03/13/06 11:31 AM	1.7318		
			03/13/06 12:21 PM		1.7301	**170.00**
021	EUR/USD	100K	03/13/06 11:43 AM	1.1940		
			03/13/06 12:54 PM		1.1937	**30.00**
624	EUR/USD	100K	03/13/06 08:10 PM	1.1967		
			03/13/06 08:16 PM		1.1962	**50.00**
288	EUR/USD	100K	03/14/06 09:58 AM	1.1984		
			03/23/06 10:29 AM		1.1978	**60.00**
061	EUR/USD	100K	03/14/06 04:52 PM	1.2010		
			03/23/06 10:28 AM		1.1988	**220.00**
256	AUD/USD	100K	03/15/06 12:21 PM	0.7380		
			03/15/06 11:49 PM		0.7374	**60.00**
408	GBP/USD	100K	03/15/06 01:26 PM	1.7462		
			03/15/06 11:46 PM		1.7457	**50.00**
712	EUR/USD	100K	03/19/06 09:20 PM	1.2174		
			03/20/06 09:51 AM		1.2163	**110.00**
549	EUR/JPY	100K	03/20/06 12:21 PM		141.49	
			03/20/06 04:54 PM	141.59		**85.93**
554	NZD/USD	100K	03/20/06 07:30 PM		0.6238	
			03/20/06 07:44 PM	0.6245		**70.00**
591	EUR/USD	100K	03/21/06 08:26 AM	1.2150		
			03/21/06 08:58 AM		1.2139	**110.00**
095	EUR/USD	100K	03/21/06 10:51 AM	1.2090		
			03/21/06 10:54 AM		1.2088	**20.00**
771	GBP/USD	100K	03/22/06 04:11 AM		1.7491	
			03/22/06 09:27 AM	1.7492		**10.00**
364	GBP/JPY	100K	03/22/06 08:00 AM	204.33		
			03/22/06 08:31 AM		204.15	**154.08**
026	USD/JPY	100K	03/22/06 10:00 AM	116.82		
			03/22/06 10:18 AM		116.72	**85.68**
034	GBP/JPY	100K	03/22/06 10:03 AM	204.27		
			03/22/06 10:23 AM		204.05	**188.65**
612	EUR/JPY	100K	03/22/06 07:31 PM	141.15		
			03/22/06 07:53 PM		141.07	**68.45**
749	USD/JPY	100K	03/22/06 08:04 PM	116.82		
			03/22/06 08:17 PM		116.77	**42.82**

FIGURE 9.2 *(Continued)*

Ticket #	Currency	Volume	Date	Sold	Bought	Gross P/L
834	EUR/USD	100K	03/22/06 08:19 PM	1.2055		
			03/23/06 10:02 AM		1.2040	**150.00**
706	AUD/USD	100K	03/23/06 01:24 PM	0.7145		
			03/23/06 03:14 PM		0.7144	**10.00**
614	USD/JPY	100K	03/23/06 06:41 PM	117.80		
			03/24/06 10:16 AM		117.79	**8.49**
677	GBP/USD	100K	03/28/06 06:31 AM	1.7476		
			03/28/06 02:21 PM		1.7470	**60.00**
724	EUR/USD	100K	03/28/06 10:05 AM	1.2078		
			03/28/06 10:44 AM		1.2073	**50.00**
859	USD/JPY	200K	03/29/06 04:09 AM		117.95	
			03/29/06 06:25 AM	118.02		**118.62**
003	USD/CAD	100K	03/29/06 05:12 AM	1.1727		
			03/29/06 08:28 AM		1.1715	**102.43**
451	USD/CAD	100K	03/29/06 07:37 AM	1.1727		
			03/29/06 08:28 AM		1.1715	**102.43**
661	GBP/USD	200K	03/29/06 08:41 AM		1.7355	
			03/29/06 11:41 AM	1.7361		**120.00**
970	GBP/USD	200K	03/29/06 09:40 AM		1.7341	
			03/29/06 11:32 AM	1.7353		**240.00**
402	EUR/USD	200K	03/30/06 06:21 AM		1.2080	
			03/30/06 06:32 AM	1.2082		**40.00**
529	GBP/USD	200K	03/31/06 10:03 AM	1.7337		
			04/02/06 11:02 PM		1.7330	**140.00**
856	USD/CAD	200K	04/04/06 01:08 PM		1.1637	
			04/04/06 07:36 PM	1.1638		**17.19**
812	GBP/USD	200K	04/05/06 01:02 AM	1.7590		
			04/05/06 01:57 AM		1.7585	**100.00**
317	GBP/USD	200K	04/05/06 08:14 AM	1.7509		
			04/05/06 10:05 AM		1.7500	**180.00**
700	GBP/USD	200K	04/05/06 10:20 AM	1.7503		
			04/05/06 10:30 AM		1.7489	**280.00**
722	EUR/USD	200K	04/05/06 10:23 AM	1.2273		
			04/05/06 10:44 AM		1.2268	**100.00**
896	GBP/USD	200K	04/05/06 10:34 AM	1.7493		
			04/07/06 07:31 AM		1.7488	**100.00**
907	USD/JPY	200K	04/05/06 10:36 AM		117.61	
			04/05/06 10:46 AM	117.62		**17.00**
509	GBP/USD	100K	04/05/06 08:07 PM	1.7512		
			04/06/06 12:45 PM		1.7508	**40.00**
071	GBP/USD	200K	04/06/06 11:55 AM	1.7498		
			04/07/06 06:23 AM		1.7497	**20.00**
396	GBP/USD	200K	04/06/06 01:27 PM	1.7500		
			04/07/06 06:15 AM		1.7498	**40.00**

(Continues)

FIGURE 9.2 *(Continued)*

Ticket #	Currency	Volume	Date	Sold	Bought	Gross P/L
209	USD/CAD	100K	04/10/06 10:50 AM		1.1470	
			04/10/06 12:59 PM	1.1472		**17.43**
301	EUR/USD	100K	04/10/06 05:02 PM		1.2112	
			04/10/06 05:47 PM	1.2114		**20.00**
223	GBP/USD	200K	04/11/06 01:51 AM		1.7442	
			04/11/06 03:33 AM	1.7451		**180.00**
593	GBP/USD	200K	04/11/06 07:46 AM		1.7426	
			04/11/06 07:57 AM	1.7433		**140.00**
601	USD/JPY	200K	04/11/06 07:51 AM	118.72		
			04/11/06 09:35 AM		118.66	**101.13**
671	EUR/USD	200K	04/11/06 08:07 AM		1.2114	
			04/11/06 09:09 AM	1.2115		**20.00**
631	EUR/JPY	200K	04/11/06 05:08 PM	143.60		
			04/11/06 06:47 PM		143.54	**101.51**
015	EUR/USD	200K	04/12/06 08:22 AM	1.2128		
			04/12/06 08:30 AM		1.2118	**200.00**
086	EUR/USD	200K	04/12/06 10:21 AM	1.2121		
			04/12/06 10:54 AM		1.2118	**60.00**
099	GBP/USD	200K	04/12/06 10:23 AM	1.7516		
			04/12/06 11:11 AM		1.7510	**120.00**
662	GBP/USD	200K	04/13/06 04:23 AM		1.7555	
			04/16/06 08:05 PM	1.7557		**40.00**
297	EUR/USD	200K	04/13/06 08:11 AM		1.2100	
			04/13/06 01:36 PM	1.2111		**220.00**
588	GBP/USD	200K	04/13/06 08:34 AM		1.7530	
			04/13/06 02:34 PM	1.7536		**120.00**
839	USD/JPY	200K	04/13/06 09:12 AM	118.80		
			04/13/06 10:18 AM		118.60	**337.27**
476	GBP/USD	100K	04/13/06 09:28 AM		1.7505	
			04/13/06 01:36 PM	1.7527		**220.00**
488	EUR/USD	100K	04/13/06 09:30 AM		1.2090	
			04/13/06 01:36 PM	1.2111		**210.00**
700	EUR/USD	200K	04/13/06 02:35 PM		1.2115	
			04/16/06 04:57 PM	1.2117		**40.00**
403	GBP/USD	200K	04/17/06 09:24 AM		1.7713	
			04/17/06 10:46 AM	1.7723		**200.00**
383	EUR/USD	200K	04/17/06 11:10 AM	1.2272		
			04/17/06 11:28 AM		1.2266	**120.00**
021	EUR/USD	200K	04/17/06 02:38 PM	1.2267		
			04/17/06 02:48 PM		1.2266	**20.00**
228	USD/CHF	200K	04/17/06 04:35 PM		1.2798	
			04/18/06 02:54 AM	1.2803		**78.11**
944	EUR/USD	200K	04/18/06 08:40 AM		1.2281	
			04/18/06 08:54 AM	1.2294		**260.00**

FIGURE 9.2 *(Continued)*

Ticket #	Currency	Volume	Date	Sold	Bought	Gross P/L
014	GBP/USD	200K	04/18/06 08:44 AM		1.7764	
			04/18/06 08:54 AM	1.7778		**280.00**
360	GBP/USD	200K	04/18/06 02:26 PM		1.7814	
			04/18/06 04:51 PM	1.7825		**220.00**
055	USD/JPY	200K	04/19/06 09:22 AM		117.71	
			04/19/06 09:23 AM	117.83		**203.68**
215	USD/CHF	200K	04/19/06 09:27 AM		1.2760	
			04/20/06 07:05 AM	1.2766		**94.00**
012	USD/CAD	200K	04/19/06 10:34 AM		1.1385	
			04/20/06 05:17 AM	1.1387		**35.13**
051	GBP/USD	200K	04/19/06 10:41 AM	1.7886		
			04/19/06 11:21 PM		1.7881	**100.00**
640	EUR/USD	100K	04/19/06 12:23 PM	1.2379		
			04/19/06 12:55 PM		1.2372	**70.00**
915	USD/CAD	200K	04/19/06 01:05 PM		1.1367	
			04/19/06 09:25 PM	1.1370		**52.77**
338	USD/CHF	300K	04/20/06 10:40 AM	1.2778		
			04/20/06 11:13 AM		1.2767	**258.48**
504	EUR/USD	300K	04/20/06 10:51 AM		1.2290	
			04/20/06 10:58 AM	1.2310		**600.00**
587	USD/CHF	100K	04/20/06 10:57 AM	1.2784		
			04/20/06 11:13 AM		1.2767	**133.16**
607	EUR/JPY	300K	04/20/06 03:44 PM	144.70		
			04/20/06 04:19 PM		144.68	**51.09**
515	GBP/USD	300K	04/20/06 07:51 PM		1.7755	
			04/20/06 07:54 PM	1.7764		**270.00**
151	GBP/USD	300K	04/20/06 08:00 PM		1.7785	
			04/20/06 08:25 PM	1.7789		**120.00**
Total:						**10,620.16**
Posted at statement period of time:						**10,620.16**

FIGURE 9.2 *(Continued)*

trading system. I had been trading before and even took another class, but I lost my margin. So far, this latest class that I took has been good to me.

"I didn't go live immediately after the training session and achieve the success that is illustrated [in Figure 9.2]. I was instructed to achieve at least 50 trades on a demo while using appropriate stops before going live. I was then instructed to only trade on a mini and prove to myself that I could handle the live markets before going on to a larger and more dangerous type of account, which is a standard account. I just began trading the live standard account because I was finally able to trade profitably and create a string of successes on a live mini account.

"I did incur losses on my live account when I first began trading it, even after having success on the demo; in fact, I incurred quite a few, but not as many losses as I had seen prior to taking a course. I had to go back to the demo numerous times, and I began to realize I needed to do more planning and add more confirmations to each entry. It seemed that on a demo I could do no wrong, but when it became a live trade, I made wrong decisions most of the time.

"I think I had losses in my live account after having success on the demo, I believe, because I suddenly realized I was trading my personal live money and that it wasn't on a demo anymore. Fortunately, I am trading successfully for the first time in my life and hope to keep improving.

"In terms of my next trading goals and strategy, I was very excited to have made a little more than $10,000 in profits from a start-up of about $2,000, and I shared my news with my mentor. He was very excited for me, but then he told me I had messed up by pushing too many entries on such a small amount of money. This does not allow for a buffer if my required stop is based on a larger time compression, and he told me I could have easily lost the entire account by placing too many entries with not enough money.

"Therefore, as he has instructed me, in the future, I have decided to have only one or two trades live per $10,000 based on a 200:1 ratio until my margin has increased to $15,000. I will then trade one or two trades, with some being two lots, until $20,000 is reached. For every $5,000 of profits that I earn in the margin, my mentor told me to consider increasing my lots, but I will never overtrade the account or place undue stress on my margin and increase risk."

What You Can Learn from This Example

Completing consecutive trades in a row without a loss is a personal goal that you should strive to achieve, because it will teach you to focus on selective trade entries, instead of following your hunches or accepting losses as if they are part of the program. It doesn't have to be this way. If you trade 25 trades and then have a loss, you should consider starting all over again on your string trading goals. It is my belief that if you achieve successful string trading, then your focus will increase as well as your margin balance. I also believe that if you have a system of trade tracking, you will focus more on achieving consecutive trades than on the balance in your account. Enjoy achieving a string of trades while using tight stops for protection, and you will develop a sense of achievement, while the margin balance will take care of itself.

CHAPTER 10

More about Extreme Levels in the Market

There are 12 levels in total related to the extreme levels (ELs) of a larger time compression. These involve the weekly, which then expands to larger time compressions and contracts to the smallest time compression known. The four levels that are considered to be the basis comprise:

- The two outer extreme levels that surround the smaller time compression trading ranges.
- The two inner wall areas that form within the two outer extreme levels.

The outer extreme levels are referred to as the top extreme and the bottom extreme levels. The inside levels are illustrated in Figure 10.1 as two inner walls, indicating a measured trading range with anywhere from 60 pips to 150 pips, depending on the currency combination.

As mentioned, extreme levels are considered the outer levels of a trading range; beyond these ELs are standard off-market levels or rates that commonly offer a reversal point within a +/– 10-pip area either above or below the off-market rate. The distance within the inner walls is where traders are most likely to lose trades while using a traditional methodology, and this is known as the "dogfight" section of the daily market. Traders trading in this area feel that they must trade every day and scalp or be a day trader, and as a result, they often begin to see trades that are not present. These mirage-type traders lose money and become part of the 80 to 90 percent of historical traders who fail.

If you can learn how to trade in this area of the inner walls profitably, then you are more likely to be successful when the market reaches the extreme levels (ELs). I

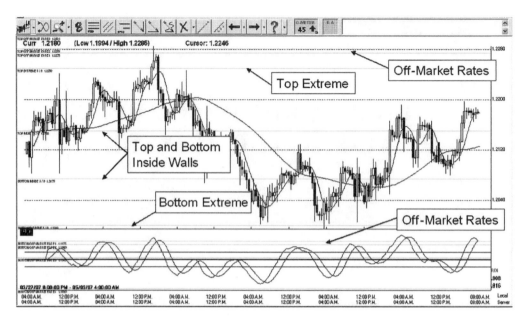

FIGURE 10.1 Top and bottom inside walls, top and bottom extremes, and off-market rates. Courtesy of Concorde Forex Group, Inc. The extreme levels are offered daily on CFGSmartCharts. They are horizontal lines automatically placed and updated on the charts.

suggest you trade several demo accounts within this area of inner walls on a daily basis to develop your personal trading skills, but save the live trades for signals that have increased odds of your making a successful entry and a profitable exit.

As mentioned earlier, the two extreme levels indicate the outer range area of an obvious overbought or oversold status, which offers traders a possible reversal or bend in the market that is most likely a predictable event. The extreme levels represent a larger trading range, with smaller trading ranges contained within. Over the years, I have noticed that this type of trading range seems to float and shift every few days with a predictive nature. If the top extreme level shifts upward, then the market seems to follow within the week or so. Because determining the direction of the market is probably the single most important consideration for each trade entry, I believe this one indicator confirms what all other signals are implying regarding direction.

Outside or beyond these outer extreme levels, we use four off-market levels for possible cost-averaging entries and/or new entries. What is unique about these outer levels—beyond the extreme levels—is that they seem to be seasonal and may change every fall or spring for no apparent reason. Another unique feature about the extreme levels, as well as about the off-market levels, is that this is the general area in which a bend in the market occurs. This type of knowledge is absolutely critical when merged with specialty forex trading signals and tools. It instantly increases your odds of having successful entries in the market.

HOW MAY TRADERS OBTAIN THESE EXTREME LEVELS?

Each day, the levels are published free (at this time) and placed on certain charts within the industry, with no obligation on the part of the technical analyst to publish. The levels appear automatically, approximately every 8 to 12 hours on each market open beginning with the London, New York, and then the Asia. The levels appear instantly to all CFG associates as well as to those members of an information vault group called the "Forex Producers." Although you may have to pay for the charting service to obtain the information, the Extreme application does not currently come with an extra charge. The author and provider of the service offer the benefit to only certain companies that qualify who then may white label the service for resale.

Currently, traders may view the chart applications for a free time period by contacting a chart provider (listed in the appendix at the end of this book). If you are an advanced trader or intermediate trader with a proven track record of profitable and successful trading history, you may qualify for membership into the Forex Producers trading group and have access to the levels through another type of charting package. The Forex Producers provides a vaulted source of information to advanced traders who are less likely to become confused with massive information.

WHAT TRADING SKILLS DO TRADERS NEED FOR TRADING EXTREMES?

Basic skills are necessary as well as an applied understanding of elementary trading skills. Basic understanding of elementary definitions would be very helpful; however, outstanding trading tools is more important. The following sections provide general definitions of trading tools typically used.

Candlestick Charting

It is recommended that traders use a charting service that has the ability to show eight time compressions at the same time on any one currency combination. The recommended time compressions are the 5-minute, 10-minute, 30-minute, one-hour, two-hour, four-hour, daily, and weekly charts for each country combination that you plan to trade. Candlestick charting as opposed to other styles of charts is recommended.

Data Feed for Tracking the Market

Many free charting services are found on the Internet; however, most of the services use only 2 to 20 banks for their data feeds, which may often be the same data that they are obtaining from their clearing firms. The feeds from these services may often be delayed or historical. Many brokers offer free charts, but sometimes that can be like swimming with sharks; in other words, the broker has access to everything you are also watching, and if the broker takes a position against you, then he (or she) can see everything you see—which could be a real negative for you, as an individual trader.

Using an outside charting service that has a mass of banks feeding real live-time data into the service is always going to offer the best advantage for individual traders. Brokers usually say bad things about independent charting companies, especially those that use more than 400 banks with fast data feed averages, because these give *traders* the edge instead of the broker. I have often wondered why broker-dealers don't just buy these types of charts and trade along with the traders when trades are in everyone's favor. Proper volumes of data, when fed into a good charting service that receives the feed in microseconds, usually update through to the charts as quickly as in just three to six seconds to achieve a virtually real-time data feed for traders. Not only is the feed used for developing the charts, it is also used to supply enough data for archiving historical information to average the feed and then create oscillators to measure the market.

River Oscillator Indicator Signals

River Oscillator Indicators (ROI signals) are two oscillating lines that allow traders to match time compressions to Fibonacci levels. Figure 10.2 shows an example.

River Channel Signals

The river channel (RC) acts as a type of volume moving average, moving within the measuring of the market, preferably through candlestick charts. When coordinated with the ROI signals and multiple time compressions, the RC signal becomes a very powerful confirmation tool. Figure 10.3 shows an example.

Multiple Time Compressions

Most charting packages will not allow traders to view eight time compressions at once. If a multiple compression chart package is available to traders, as shown in Figure 10.4, it will give you the necessary overall quick view of Fib comparisons, as well as a

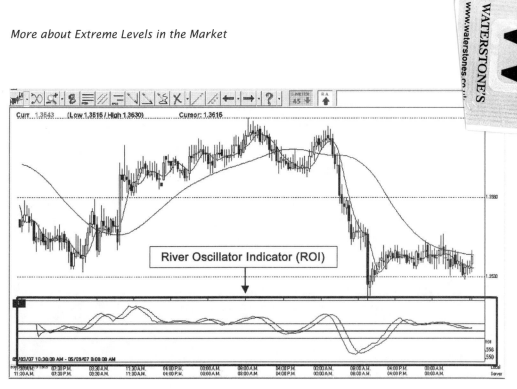

FIGURE 10.2 River Oscillator Indicator (ROI signal).
Courtesy of Concorde Forex Group, Inc.

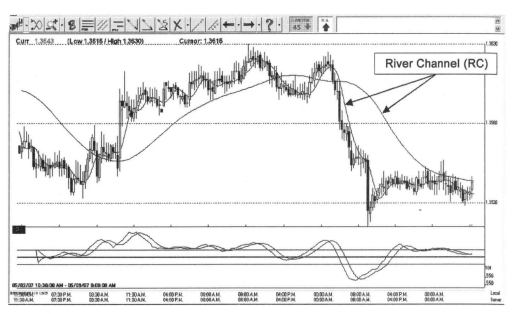

FIGURE 10.3 River channel (RC) signal.
Courtesy of Concorde Forex Group, Inc.

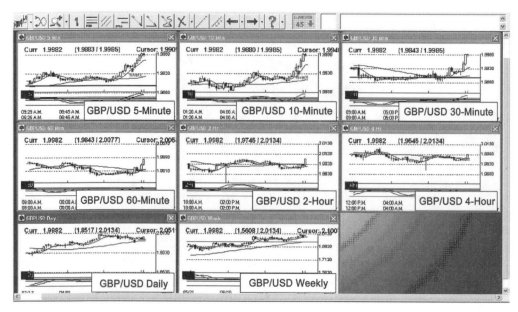

FIGURE 10.4 Multiple time compressions.
Courtesy of Concorde Forex Group.

quick confirming glance at ROIs, RCs, slow stochastic measurements, and other volume indicators.

Multiple time compressions also allow traders to view a possible Fib 1.27 reversal point when associated with extreme levels and trend-wall crashes when time is critical for an entry. A 1.27 is an all-time high or low, and when all time compressions have the same number for a high or low. When 1.27 tops or bottoms all match at the same time, we begin looking very quickly for other reasons to confirm a possible reversal entry in the market.

Automated Trend-Tracking Software

There's no guessing required with automated trend-tracking software systems. This type of software, found on some charting packages, allows ongoing adjustments for identification of trends due to constantly changing market conditions. Very few charting packages allow viewers to have access to floating trend lines within the trends. Automated trend-tracking software, such as that shown in Figure 10.5, allows you to view reversal trends within a larger trend; when the two trend walls clash, the reversal in the direction of the overall trend where both trend signals agree becomes a new entry. These new entries do require additional confirmations from other volume indicators.

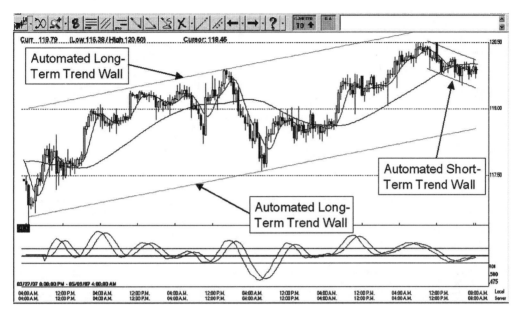

FIGURE 10.5 Automated trend-tracking software: long-term and short-term trend walls. Courtesy of Concorde Forex Group, Inc.

STRATEGY FOR TRADING INSIDE THE WALLS OF THE S90/CROSSOVER

As the market approaches the top or bottom inner walls of a trading range, the S90/Crossovers that are associated with these range levels offer an easy choice for beginners as well as more advanced traders. Without some sort of guidelines, such as the extreme levels, a new trader (or even an advanced trader) must find some sort of rules and confirmations to be followed to avoid unnecessary losses.

Millions of levels are available to traders in the forex within trading ranges—and within trading ranges found within trading ranges that are compounded, it seems, into infinity. Choosing a safe and correct level for a planned entry and then following the plan with no emotion has become a major challenge for many traders because of the massive amount of information that has suddenly appeared on the Internet in just the past few years. It is difficult for traders to determine what system or program to follow that will give the best protection for their margin accounts.

Figures 10.6 through 10.9 are simple reversal entry examples in which the market moved to the extreme level and then bounced off of the level, indicating an entry point. The arrows in Figures 10.6 through 10.9 reveal the profit possibilities. Even great trade examples must have additional confirmations such as the ROI found at the bottom of

FIGURE 10.6 Reversal entry example: 60-pip movement.
Courtesy of Concorde Forex Group.

FIGURE 10.7 Reversal entry example: 100-pip movement.
Courtesy of Concorde Forex Group, Inc.

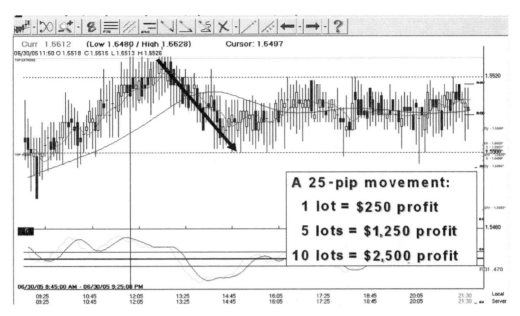

FIGURE 10.8 Reversal entry example: 25-pip movement.
Courtesy of Concorde Forex Group, Inc.

FIGURE 10.9 Reversal entry example: 100-pip movement.
Courtesy of Concorde Forex Group, Inc.

FIGURE 10.10 Example of a sideways market within the top and bottom inside walls.
Courtesy of Concorde Forex Group, Inc.

Figures 10.6 through 10.9, in which case the two oscillating lines have crossed down or
up in the direction of the reversal entry.

In Figures 10.10 and 10.11, a battle zone area is often found daily within the inner
walls. This area is where most lamb markets or consolidations occur as the market
moves sideways. Many traders feel they must trade every day as day traders, and within
the inner walls is where their money is lost. Selective trading techniques will help you
avoid risky scenarios.

Found within these inner wall levels are basic Fibonacci levels of .618, .50, and .382,
as marked within the spaces in Figure 10.12.

WHEN THE MARKET MOVES CLOSER TO THE LEVEL

If you are using the proper software, then you may have an option to be alerted by the
charting software for trade opportunities 24 hours a day. When you receive an alert,
you should always inspect the alert and then confirm the opportunity before making a
decision to enter the market. Always have a predetermined stop in mind as well as a
profit limit to enjoy.

FIGURE 10.11   Example of a sideways market within the top and bottom inside walls.
Courtesy of Concorde Forex Group, Inc.

FIGURE 10.12   Illustration of Fibonacci levels within the top and bottom inside walls.
Courtesy of Concorde Forex Group, Inc.

The ROI or other momentum-type software is normally found below the chart compression. The oscillator should not only be calibrated to identify entry points that you must learn to interpret; it should also allow you to determine exit points as well. The stochastic oscillator may be significant in determining the validity of the trade, because it will recalibrate prematurely as a reversal indicating a trade exit; however, profit pips will be left on the table. Most of the charts in this book will not have a stochastic oscillator to view, and the trades displayed will rely on the ROI because it allows you to view maximized profits. Interpretation is not something that you can learn from a book; developing interpretation skills comes with time, practice, patience, and perseverance.

In Figure 10.13, the lower extreme from May 24, 2005, was reached on the GBP$ (British pound) at 1.8250 and breached by only 5 pips, which justifies the reason for a tight protective stop rather than using a large stop or no stop, as some traders do. The market so far has reached 1.8279, offering 29 pips of movement or $290 net per lot, because the broker is supposedly paid on entry through a predetermined small spread.

Notice the ROI position as the market tapped the lower extreme level. The ROI has broken upward, acting as a confirmation for the bull bounce entry. The upper oscillator in Figure 10.13 is a standard stochastic for comparison and is used as a confirmation as well. The traditional slow stochastic oscillator does not always agree with the ROI, but when it does, it serves as a confirmation source; however, the ROI and other volume

FIGURE 10.13 Illustration of a bull bounce in the British pound.
Courtesy of Concorde Forex Group, Inc.

indicators have never served as a confirmation source for the slow stochastic by anyone I have ever interviewed.

In Figure 10.14, two extreme levels were hit on the NZD$ (New Zealand dollar): Not marked on the left is the April 27, 2005, lower extreme as found on the lower horizontal line. The .7200 bottom strike was followed by a market move over the next two days to a top of .7350, which offered a 150-pip range of profit potential, and then returned to the comfort zone of the inner range. The letter *S* that appears on the bottom left-hand side of this particular smart-type chart indicates that information about this extreme strike is found in the signal icon at the top of the chart.

Two weeks later the NZD$ top extreme moved exactly to .7150 and then fell to .7107, offering 43 pips of positive movement to traders, as shown in Figure 10.15.

The NZD$ upper extreme level became a 1.27 entry down, as shown in Figure 10.16. The combination exceeded the extreme by only 5 pips but is offering the trader an easy 25 pips thus far per lot.

The NZD$ upper extreme bear trade moved 32 pips to .7343 from the .7375 extreme level, thus far breached by only 4 pips to .7379. Here, we've already exited and are now waiting to see if the combination becomes a .786 at .7375 for another bear trade. Another tight stop was used in the trade with the margin going negative only 4 pips before moving into profits. Notice the ROI oscillator right after the extreme strike shown in Figure 10.17.

Figure 10.18 shows how a proprietary alert signal on the SmartCharts generated a buy signal (RiverX) when the market went to the top inside wall. This illustration offers

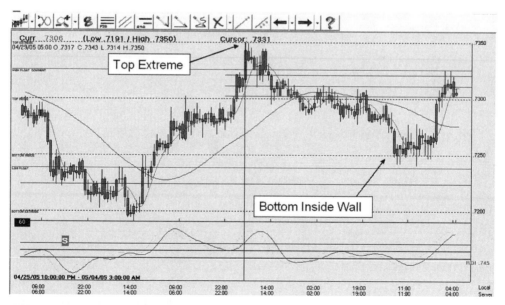

FIGURE 10.14 A reversal entry opportunity after an extreme market strike at 1.8320 level. Courtesy of Concorde Forex Group, Inc.

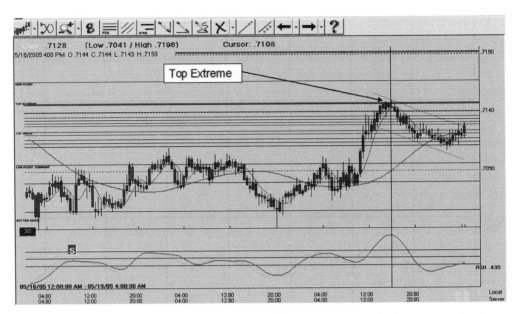

FIGURE 10.15 A view of how the market tends to bend as a reversal when extreme levels are reached.
Courtesy of Concorde Forex Group, Inc.

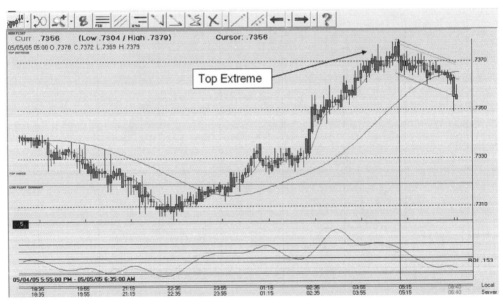

FIGURE 10.16 An extreme strike allows use of very tight stops providing the ROI is in agreement.
Courtesy of Concorde Forex Group, Inc.

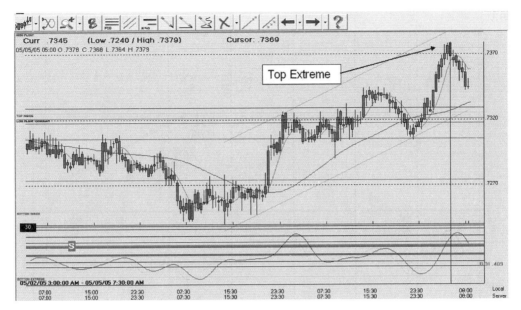

FIGURE 10.17 The market moved upward to the extreme as a buy target with ROI agreement regarding direction. Once the level made the strike, then a reversal sell opportunity is available with the beginning of a ROI down X agreement.
Courtesy of Concorde Forex Group, Inc.

FIGURE 10.18 A buy target and then a sell entry on the upper exteme with a confirmation signal known as a RiverX proprietary buy signal, implying that the software is encouraging either a first entry if not already in or a chance to add lots to an existing trade.
Courtesy of Concorde Forex Group, Inc.

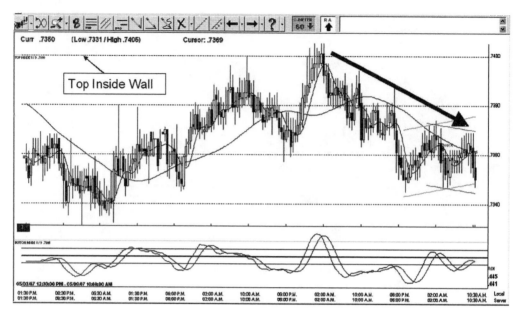

FIGURE 10.19 A strike on an inner wall. In this particular case, the inner wall had been at a historical extreme level for many months and only traders using the smart chart service would have known that this history existed. Duplicated levels have historical value and may offer reversals as long as multiple time compression ROI confirmations exist.
Courtesy of Concorde Forex Group, Inc.

the same identical opportunity for a buy target and then a sell entry on the upper exteme as found in Figure 10.17, but with a confirmation signal. Although it breached the inner wall, once the ROI turned down, the combination made the reversal. Obviously, the RiverX is a signal that should be considered as an entry point.

Finally, Figure 10.19 shows how the NZD/USD reacted off of the top inside wall. The market fell 50 pips.

CHAPTER 11

When to Bail Out of the Trade and When to Stay In for Additional Profits

As I said in the Introduction, "The greatest distance to overcome in each trade is found between the ears."

Every trader has experienced a trade where maybe you see a few pips of profit as you trade toward a legitimate profit target, and suddenly the trade begins to move against you. The logic in your brain tells you the target is a good one and the entry was a perfect entry point, so why is this trade going against you? As the indicators become more and more negative as the loss is quickly approaching your protective stop, panic begins to settle in. You reason that the target is good and that all you have to do is to move the stop a little further. Of course, then the market moves even faster toward your stop, and your reasoning power suggests that you should move the stop to an even greater area of protection, risking even more of the margin. If the market does turn back toward your original limit, which may take hours or even days to surrender, most traders are so happy to see even a small profit that they will escape the trade with only one to five pips of profit. The problem is the market was chasing you (the trader) on the wrong side of the trade, instead of you chasing the market on the profit side.

So get it straight between your ears before you lose your entire margin. Calculate a stop and stick to it, right or wrong! You can always get back into the trade and make your money back if a loss occurs. Failing to get back on the horse quickly is a mistake that many traders make when they fall off the horse, so to speak, or make a loss.

Safety is the primary focus of a professional trader with the risk- return ratio always in mind. Normally, a resistance is formed if an upward-trending market is approaching an extreme, which will bend the market either suddenly or gradually as a reversal. Of course, if the market is bearish, then a support will form when the market reverses.

When this happens, a stop is placed just above the resistance (about five to seven pips above the high) and if bearish, then the stop would be placed five to seven pips below the new support.

A reversal entry from an extreme must have other confirmations of either a traditional or a modern signal to indicate a confirmation. As Figure 11.1 implies, a tight stop of less than 20 pips is all that is necessary, with potential profits much greater than the risk.

Breaching the extreme level means that traditional and modernistic signals will not appear to justify a reversal entry. The next off-market rate to consider viewing a possible entry is located 25 pips beyond an extreme. If the 25 level is breached, then we will look at the 31st pip beyond the extreme for signals to begin appearing. Beyond the 31st, 51 pips becomes the next target, and then 101 to 105 pips for the reversal to be considered. These pip extensions beyond the extremes offer potential areas that have been historically shown as approximate reversal areas that will offer traditional or modernistic signal confirmations.

Conclusion: Who cares if you are trading a simple procedure as long as it helps pay the bills?

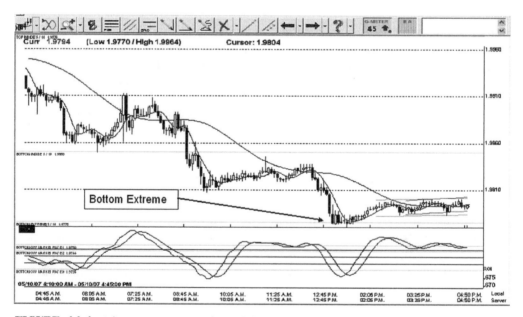

FIGURE 11.1 A bottom extreme strike and the market only breached the level by approximately 3 pips of negative before beginning its move upward. This stop would have been as small as 7 pips due to the ROI X up that occurred at the same time as the extreme strike.
Courtesy of Concorde Forex Group, Inc.

PAY THE DUES OF TIME AND PRACTICE

As I said in the Introduction, "You must persevere in the market, never giving up while learning and paying the dues of time."

Learning to trade the forex can sometimes be a very dangerous business for neophytes—which includes those traders with a lot of experience from other markets who are now entering the forex for the very first time. After years of introducing people to the forex, I have found the most successful traders began their new experience by easing into the industry with extreme caution. There is an easing-into-the-experience procedure that is recommended at Concorde Forex Group (CFG), which is to have someone guide you through the procedures of learning how to enter a trade with multiple confirmations. It takes up to two years to become really fluent with the skills of selective trading, which enables you to walk away from a trade that does not meet the requirements to be profitable. It's true that some people grasp the concepts faster than others and begin achieving success almost immediately; however, give yourself the benefit of the doubt and assume that you have something to learn at all times.

Most traders I have met began a trading career with the intention to become independent enough to eventually become full-time traders at home with no need to deal with the public. I have worked with approximately 5,000 traders who began careers as neophytes, and every one of them had a desire to chase the "pie in the sky" or had a get-rich-quick attitude. The survivors would eventually realize that trading is not an easy task and that it takes time, patience, a positive mental attitude, proper margin funding, and accepting personal responsibility for their own decisions in the market.

A professional trader and one of my personal mentors from Switzerland once told me, "For a beginning trader, it is as easy and quick to lose $1,000 in the market as it is to lose $100,000." He also said, "A good trader with patience and proper selections of trade entries can make $1,000,000 with $1,000 as well as with $100,000." When I became a mentor and began to help traders learn the forex, I saw a young trader take a $500 mini account margin to $15,000 in about 30 days, and I also have seen other traders take a $500 mini account margin to $50 in one day. What's the difference? Selective trading skills were developed along with the patience to wait, watch, and pay the dues of time with lots of practice on a demo.

Suggestion: After proving to yourself that you can trade successfully on a demo, then begin with a small margin investment and ease into the world of live trading by opening a live mini account. It's a lot different, psychologically, trading a live account as opposed to a demo account, and most beginning traders become very discouraged when finally going live after having tremendous success with a demo. Most beginning traders that I have met have some success on a demo without using stops with a large margin of $50,000 or more, and then they open small accounts with only $500 to $1,000 and expect the same results. Even if they are told in a classroom setting about the necessity of using stops, they continue to go live too soon and have unnecessary losses.

A simple approach to entering a trade with a confirmation to consider may be the one described next.

INSTRUCTIONS FOR A SIMPLE TRADE

This trade is not a perfect trade, but if traded on the major currencies and stops are used to avoid unnecessary losses, it may be very helpful for you to consider as one of your primary trade entries. It is called a sore thumb (ST) trade entry. The ST trade entry is fairly easy to recognize, but it needs to have some confirmations to go with it, such as a volume indicator or a River Oscillator Indicator (ROI) pushing in the same direction, because the ST implies that the market is going to move in the opposite direction of the spike or large wick in the near future. Larger time compressions may be the best to trade from, because larger volume is visually apparent.

An ST is formed when the market moves quickly in one direction and then pulls back as a result of a quick reversal in the market, as illustrated in Figure 11.2. The pullback creates a visually obvious wick, or spike, that stands out in appearance from the other

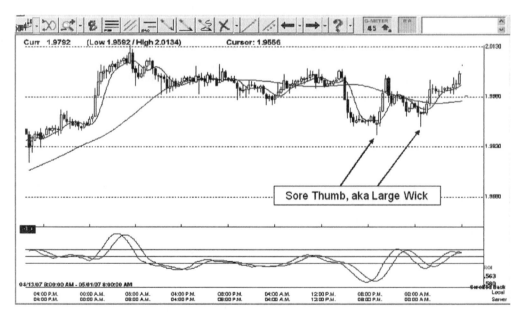

FIGURE 11.2 Example of a sore thumb (ST) trade entry.
Courtesy of Concorde Forex Group, Inc.

candles. Once the ST trade entry is made and a stop is placed in the proper position, provided the volume oscillator indicators agree, then you should begin looking for gaps as well as S90/Crossovers for a possible profit target.

HAVE A PLAN AND TRADE THE PLAN

Although there is much confusion on the Internet regarding just how much the foreign currency exchange actually produces per day, one thing is certain: The forex is a very large and volatile business for entrepreneurial traders to become involved in. Every entrepreneur I have ever met has always had a plan with short-range as well as long-range goals.

Here are three examples of having a plan.

Example 1

Trade 15 trades with one lot per trade, per week, for 10 pips, with an average profit of $10 per trade; 150 pips per week at $10 equals $1,500 per week.

Let's add a vacation, as in the next example.

Example 2

Some would say this example is the goal of a part-time trader:

- Trade 10 points a day.
- The broker pays an average $10 a point (pip) = $100 per day.
- Trade five days per week = $500 per week.
- Trade 40 weeks a year (includes a three-month vacation).
  - Trade one lot per day = $20,000 per year.
  - Trade five lots per day = $100,000 per year.
  - Trade 10 lots per day = $200,000 per year.

Beginning with one lot is the best approach to develop the long-term discipline described in this book. As you develop personal trading skills, it would not be a good idea to just jump into five lots. It should be a gradual reward system; once you've accumulated enough margin, then promote yourself to trading two lots, then three, and so on.

How much needs to be in the margin account before you promote yourself to the next level? There are many different opinions on just how much should be in a margin account per lot trade and just exactly what the risk/reward ratio should be on any given trade. I will offer a few suggestions for you to consider. I am sure that most traders will come up with their own personal opinions and criteria to follow. After all, risk tolerance is a personal and individual decision that all traders must make. This means you must come to a personal conclusion as to just how much you are willing to allow a trade to go into the negative before bailing out.

Now let's take a look at the potential of a full-time professional trader.

Example 3

This example involves only one currency combination with focus and selective trading. We will assume that the trader is trading only the $JPY (Japanese yen) on a standard account, with the goal to obtain 100 pips per lot per week.

Pick one or develop your own plan. Start small with only two to four trades per week and set a goal to develop into a 40-lot trader. The example that follows is based on obtaining 100 pips per lot per week and the $JPY paying an average of $8.50 per pip.

100 pips with 1 lot × $8.50 = $850 per week.
100 pips with 2 lots × $8.50 = $1,700 per week.
100 pips with 3 lots × $8.50 = $2,550 per week.
100 pips with 4 lots × $8.50 = $3,400 per week.
100 pips with 5 lots × $8.50 = $4,250 per week.
100 pips with 10 lots × $8.50 = $8,500 per week.
100 pips with 15 lots × $8.50 = $12,750 per week.
100 pips with 20 lots × $8.50 = $17,000 per week.
100 pips with 30 lots × $8.50 = $25,500 per week.

The long-term goal is to obtain 100 pips with 40 lots × $8.50 = $34,000 per week × 40 weeks = $1,360,000 potential gross with 12 weeks off for vacation.

Final Thoughts

- Make sure you trade demo or play money successfully before moving into the world of live trading.
- Once you are ready to trade live, then consider trading on a live mini account with a very small amount of deposited margin to ease into the world of live trading.
- It is not only an emotional learning experience to gain control of but sometimes a very stressful event in your life to move from trading demo money to live money.
- Once you have achieved success with a small live mini account, then move on to the larger standard accounts where risk becomes greater as well as potential profits.
- Consider focusing on one currency combo and become a specialist at that before spreading yourself thin trying to learn about other combinations. Yen combinations are interesting. Starting with the $Yen and then moving on to the EURJPY, and so on, may offer more benefits in terms of gradual skill development than you can imagine. This type of approach can intensify your focus and increase the odds of your success as a trader.
- When and if you become extremely successful, people may appear in your life offering you a lot of money to trade for them, and if you accept and are not properly licensed with all the necessary extended schooling, then you may find yourself going on a free federal vacation: to prison.
- In other words, you are learning to trade your own money and not someone else's.

I feel that great traders have often found a simple trade and have had the discipline to stick with it. No merging of other techniques or personally unproven styles are allowed into their minds once they have discovered the secret simple trade and implemented it successfully on a daily basis.

I have always said a mentor is a guide. The real mentor is found by spending personal time, as an individual, in the market and by developing a maturity that requires time, patience, and sometimes a lot of money. Therefore, spend a lot of time trading on a free demo and save the special good-looking trading opportunities for the live account.

When failure or a loss occurs, pointing a finger at someone else or a particular methodology is the loser's way. Not forgetting where you come from as well as accepting personal responsibility for personal decisions in the market separates a *real* trader from the wannabe trader. It separates the winner from a whiner. Always have a winner's attitude and be happy every time you enter the market.

Stay in the river,
Don

Selections from CFG Newsletters

PERIPHERAL TRADING IN THE FOREX MARKET

Often traders, especially neophytes, allow emotions to take over and rule the rules of trading. This usually produces failure, and the trader leaves the forex industry with losses, never to come back. Some will come to their senses and begin following strict rules for selective entries while using tight stops. After all, I have said many times, "The greatest distance to travel in the forex is found between the ears."

I have seen over and over in the lives of many neophyte traders that they experience the same agony of loss by going live too soon. However, some accept responsibility for their actions in the market and move on to success by not giving up. Enduring the test of time and paying the dues of time in the market is obviously one of the burdens that all beginners have to experience.

What is peripheral trading? Peripheral trading is what I refer to as a type of awareness that traders need to have when entering or exiting a trade. To solve the problem of unawareness in the markets, you should become aware of how to identify certain critical levels in the market that usually create a bend or a reversal. As most traders know, there are Fibonacci levels within trading ranges that could be identified into infinity, and the larger the trading range, the larger the number of identifiable levels of historical Fibonacci levels that are established during former trading ranges. The levels are referred to as the S90/Crossovers, inner/outer walls, and extreme levels, with their off-market rate levels. When conditions are right in the market, and if the market approaches one of these mathematical and visually identified special levels, then modernistic as well as some traditional signals often begin to appear. This is one of the most important confirmation procedures that some backroom traders use to select an entry.

As an example, if the market is approaching an extreme level and if conditions are right, then you will notice a reversal. A modernistic wave trade will appear if the market is going to make a significant move. Also, other modern trade identification procedures and systems such as bridges, River Channel Up/River Channel Down (RCU/RCD) extension clusters, river bend trades, and other confirming signals may be present. These duplicating confirmations and the awareness of the presence of other confirmations will only increase the safety of the trade as well as give you, the trader, an edge in the market.

Summary: The greater the number of various types of confirmations that appear, the greater the odds of a successful and profitable trade. Memorizing more than 10 different types of forex signature trades, procedures, and their associated signals, as well as practicing them on a demo until proficient, will only enhance the probability of your success when trading the largest legal financial industry in the world, the forex.

DAILY TRADING TIPS

Traders may feel a need to trade every day, probably due to a need to succeed or pay the bills. This urgency to succeed or to pay the bills by trading every possible minute often leads to mistakes in the market. Making trades happen (i.e., forcing them) instead of allowing a trade to come to you leads to failure; market opportunities must come to traders naturally as market conditions allow. Waiting for a trade opportunity to develop may force you to take a day or two off from entries until conditions in the market shape up properly.

The time taken off by traders during the waiting periods, if you have limited yourself to only one or two combinations, will allow you to spend time with personal studies. Others, who have expanded their forex trading portfolio to include numerous country combinations, have more opportunity and will find themselves busy enough to eventually become full-time traders, if they're not already trading full-time. It seems there is opportunity in the forex marketplace almost 24 hours a day, if you have the proper tools to assist in alerting you of possible entries into the market.

Work Smart and Not Hard

If you use the CFGSmartCharts or other similar charting systems, then you will be able to monitor the multiple River Oscillator Indicators (ROIs) found at the bottom of the charts while using the automated notification software for time-compression agreements. This will cut down on the time needed in front of your computer screen for the best alerts if trading Cherry-type trades, ROI trades, and other types of modernistic signature trades. (A Cherry-type trade is a trade with a high percentage chance that it will be successful. An example would be as follows: If a trader views a ROI strike on a .50 level on a time compression with at least three other, different, time compressions revealing a fib strike on different fib levels with a RC X and all pointing in the same direction—then an entry of this type would carry a lower degree of risk.)

The signal icon found at the top of the charts allows you to set the other alarms to alert you when your favorite trade type appears. Signals on any software system are not guaranteed; however, they are great market watchers to alert you that maybe something is about to happen in the market. These alerts allow you to pull the chart up for proper verification before you commit to an entry, thus reducing your risk of failure.

Monitor Several Time Compressions at One Time

If you have the ability to use a PCI- or ROI-type of oscillator, there are several settings that you may use to coordinate with a Fibonacci level. For example, when a Fib strike is made at a .50 level, then you would check to see if other multiple Fib-level strikes are occurring on other time compressions. When two moving average lines are coordinated or synchronized properly with a PCI (percentage chance indicator) or an ROI, then you should easily be able to compare time-compression Fibonaccis. Traders who use SmartCharts trading software have the display already set to visually observe these types of time-compression Fib comparisons.

TRADING TIPS AND THOUGHTS

- *Confirm your possible trade entries well in advance.* A spontaneous decision to enter a trade will increase your risk of failure unless you initiate confirmations. If you make spontaneous trade entries without multiple confirmations, you may achieve some success for a while, but it takes a well-planned confirmation process to achieve 50, 100, or 200+ trades in a row without sustaining a loss. Achieving ongoing trading success takes patience. Spend time in the market observing failures and successes. Make every effort to re-create the positives. Avoid failures like the plague.
- *Plan your trade and trade your plan.* This is the best approach for trading. Brokers don't like scalpers!
- *Have a bird-dog system.* Using trading software alerts or eavesdropping on other professional live traders to see what they are doing in the market (especially if they are really good traders) may help increase your odds of success if you are a beginner or intermediate trader. I am not saying that you should trade someone else's potential trade; instead, I am suggesting you use that person as a bird dog to point out potential trades; then it is up to each individual trader (that means *you*) to use confirmations to make your final determination to enter the market—or not. Becoming proficient with your tools will aid in your interpretation and will help you to be more aware

of potential trades. Once you've been alerted and made personal confirmations, then you can decide whether to enter the trade.

A bird-dog spotting system—whether it is through another trader, a group of traders, or alert-type software—is especially good if you cannot look at 15 different currencies at one time. I certainly am not able to watch all currencies at once; therefore, I have become an expert at utilizing a smart-type charting service with alert signals to my advantage.

- *Treat trading just as you would a regular job.* Have a work schedule and stick to it. Work on being positive, and avoid all negative issues. Take responsibility for your actions in the market, and learn from your losses as well as your successes.
- *Avoid getting caught in what I call the Skype or chat room traps.* I have seen and interviewed formerly successful traders. When we analyzed when they stopped making profits, it always led back to association and meetings with unsuccessful traders. They had spent time talking to other traders (who sounded successful but weren't) at conventions, at trade shows, or in chat rooms. Traders sometimes compare their ratios of progress or success with other traders, and they become depressed because they have not succeeded.

I have witnessed too many incidents like this. In the beginning of my own trading career, I also compared my personal skill development to the progress of others, and I began to have the same failure results. To stop this path of associated failure, I had to start associating with successful traders and reading positive, success-oriented books. If you're looking for advice, you might find it in the Bible, in Galatians 6:4, which basically states that one should not compare oneself to others and that each person must be responsible for his or her own burdens. This may suggest that one is responsible for all decisions and actions taken in the market as well as the results that may occur.

KNOW THE "WWW" OF A TRADE

People often ask me what the "WWW" of a trade means. I am big on Ws because they have reminded me to keep on the right track over my years of trading. I use the Ws to remind me to keep my priorities straight on every trade entry.

The First W: *Why?*

Ask yourself the following five questions and make sure you understand the answers:

1. Why am I a trader?
2. Why I should be a trader?

3. Why is it so positive and enjoyable to be a trader?

4. Why should I trade the forex exclusively and bypass the other markets?

5. Why should anyone help someone else learn to trade?

My own reasoning is that it would be important to build the credibility of the industry and establish that there is indeed a future in trading. The fact that the forex is the largest financial industry in the world certainly helps build the case. The freedom, the happiness, the development of self-discipline, the opportunity to help others learn to trade, the opportunity to have excess funds to give to favorite charities, and the job security are all part of my answer to the first W, *why*. I must develop the attitude that I have a personal cause to be a trader and a mentor in order to constantly strive to achieve success. I want to be the knight in shining armor who comes to save the day to help others. I must feel that I have a mission to achieve. It is very important to have goals that help others. By helping others achieve success, the helper also continues to improve.

The Second W: *What?*

What do I get out of being a trader?

As a trader, you can achieve personal satisfaction, because you are calling all the shots when you make entries and exits in the markets. Becoming self-employed is a great day, as you begin to enjoy independence with no employer giving orders and no time schedule. You have the opportunity to earn money with no limits attached—enough money to help others financially, including your church, needy organizations, and victims of disasters.

The Third W: *When?*

When should I become a full-time or professional trader?

It may be one of the biggest mistakes you could make to delay learning a business that offers probably the greatest opportunity of personal financial growth in the world with a very small amount of start-up capital required. The idea is for you to invest the least amount of money with the greatest earning power. The ongoing overhead of trading the forex is very low, and your goal is to keep trade losses small while you maximize profits and implement a style of selective trade entries. With this goal achieved, then profits should grow as well as your financial freedom.

STRING TRADING

I introduced string trading to the world of forex in 1999, after my seven mentors told me it was impossible to make more than 10 trades in a row without a loss. Back then, I did exactly what my mentors told me to do, and it seemed that as soon as I hit 10 successful trades in a row, I would suddenly have an unexpected loss. This problem had to stop, because the loss usually ate up all of the profits from the previous 10 successful trades.

An acquaintance of mine (a famous speaker and author) stated, "The problem was between my ears and not between the entries." I became a selective trader in the market. I focused on string trading, but not at the risk of the margin. If I made a bad decision in the market, it was better to exit or let the market hit my stop and lose the string. Otherwise, I might suffer the loss of profits or the possible loss of an entire margin account. It is always easy to start another string. As you perfect the focus of proper entry selection in the market, you will begin to realize more profits with fewer losses.

Developing a string also encourages traders to focus on success. It is a way of developing a focus in the market. As long as you use a stop and never remove your committed stop, then when a loss occurs, you won't lose all of the profit gains that you made during your string of successful trades.

Yes, it is possible to trade 50, 100, and even 200+ trades in a row while using reasonable and often tight protective stops with a focus on increased profits.*

AUTHOR CONTACT

Contact the author of this book at Don@SelectiveForexTrading.com with questions regarding the content of this book, as well as suggestions regarding determining the differences between a real mentorship program and one that lives off of mentorship fees with no ongoing support for its trading students.

---

*__Disclaimer:__ Trading the foreign exchange market carries a high level of risk and may not be suitable for all investors. Before deciding to trade the foreign exchange market, you should carefully consider your investment objectives, level of experience, and risk appetite. The possibility exists that you could sustain a loss of some or all of your initial investment; therefore, you should not invest money that you cannot afford to lose. You should be aware of all the risk associated with foreign currency exchange trading, and you should seek advice from an independent financial advisor if you have any doubts.

A Mechanical and Nonemotional Style of Trading for Part-Time Traders

One of the greatest challenges for any trader is learning how to trade without experiencing the emotional stress of failed trades. Even when traders enter what seems to be a legitimate trade, it will occasionally go bad almost immediately. The most common reaction of an emotional trader is to just stare at the screen hoping that the trade will become positive. The correct procedure is to exit the trade based on a personal stop tolerance and then implement a plan to either reenter the trade as a cost-average entry or flip the position in order to take back the lost profits.

But what about part-time traders who need both to manage their emotions and to have a strategy that allows them to trade on a very compressed time frame? I have created a mechanical procedure for very busy people. To follow is a written explanation of this strategy. I have also included a second simple trade that I hope will increase your odds of success.

THE STRATEGY

Entries and Limits

When I am not available to monitor trades, I trade only $JPY and EURJPY combinations because I find the rate of success to be higher than for other combos using this strategy. I enter at least two separate entries each time a trade signal sounds. Trade one is for 20 pips of profit per lot, as is trade two; however, if I am close to a computer and the market is approaching the limit, then I remove the limit order for the second entry and let it ride.

One great aspect of this trade is that it provides immediate gratification—allowing one to more easily hold on to the longer-duration trade. When entry one exits with 20 pips of profit, the positive emotion justifies your being a little more relaxed about the second trade. When the first trade exits, I move my stop to zero (even) or 1 pip of profit on the second trade. This reduces exposure and risk.

In my experience, number two trade entries have often reversed, giving me only 1 pip per lot of profit. But that is better than losing money. Also, when these trades work out and miss the stop, it is wonderful to see the trade go 30, 40, and even 50 plus pips higher. Now the exit becomes the reversal ROI X that you originally based the trade entry on. Bottom line: If I am unable to remove the trade two limit because I am away from the computer, then I have two winning trades for a total of 40 pips per lot.

A Third Trade

When a signal appears in the direction of the overall trend after a major reversal is completed, I will also enter a third trade. With this trade, I have no emotional ties because I plan to make my profits from the first two entries as just described. I often find that it is emotion that drives the exit of the second trade—caused by not wanting to lose all of those fresh profits. Therefore, the third entry, which I refer to as the "I don't care trade," just moves into the world's money. I let it run until the four-hour ROI X acts as a reversal. This same strategy can be used on larger time compressions for long-term trades.

Stops

I use the automated R3/S4 found on SmartCharts to evaluate the closest support or resistance, depending on the direction of the trade. Also, the Fibonacci levels may influence the placement of a stop. As an example, assume you are trading down; if a R3 resistance is close to a .50 or .382 level from a previous trading range, then I would consider placing the stop above both the resistance and the Fib line as long as it is above the R3. Now, let's add something else to the equation: What about clusters? If a cluster is located in about the same area, then I would consider this as a confirmation. Also, one other point: Always check the river line. If using SmartCharts, then the river line is found within the flow of the candlesticks, acting similarly to a slow-moving average line indicator. If this line is above the adversity in the market as it is going against your entry, then you want to be above that line as well.

See Figures B.1 through B.19.

FIGURE B.1 USDCHF ST: This 30-minute time compression illustration offers an ST (sore thumb) with ROI confirmation regarding direction, but will be short-lived due to the downward curl that is about to occur. The ST gave a range of approximately 74 pips before danger signs of a pullback. The upper ST, as illustrated with an agreeing ROI, is about to occur very soon. The down entry in the near future will have to be delayed until the ROI has turned down. Depending on present overall trend, a possible entry may be considered if agreement with an overall down trend as determined by much larger compressions.

FIGURE B.2 EURCAD ST: This two-hour chart illustrates an ST on the top side with an ROI agreement going down. The entry is the next candle open as long as the ROI is fresh and wide, which implies that heavier volume is present. The market moved down approximately 107 pips, as illustrated by a dark bear candle. It then pulled back, forming a new ST on the bottom side, which is not seen in the illustration; however, for the ST to form, we know that a dark candle formed almost to the bottom low within the two-hour time period. The assumption now is that when the ROI crosses up, after maybe two or three more candles have appeared, a new entry will possibly appear with reduced risk and with a relatively tight stop using the former low as a support and with the stop below the support level. Of course after the ROI makes a new signal X upward, additional confirmations will be needed to justify the entry.

FIGURE B.3   EURJPY ST: Although the 421-pip move that followed the illustrated ST was in agreement with the ROI, the real lesson may be the ST found at the top of this two-hour chart on the bottom side of the market, just before the lengthy fall. Look closely and see if you can see the unmarked ST. It is pointed down and is very long—implying the market is ready to move upward—but the currency moved downward. If you look closely, you will see down below that the ROI is moving down and not up, which is not in agreement with the implied future direction of the market. Therefore, this trade would not have been entered based on an ST. Some may say that there are other reasons to enter here; however, the focus of this book is safe entries and a methodology that encourages very selective trade entries.

FIGURE B.4 GBPJPY ST: This GBPJPY four-hour chart provides a lot more profit, it seems, than most combinations. Caution is needed when trading exotic combos such as the GBPJPY, because anomalies in the market may sometimes occur against entries very suddenly. Once traders experience one of these sudden events, they will understand the value of protective stops. In this particular illustration, the combo turned out to be very safe. Both the ROI and the river line—represented by the top line in the candles or slow average—are in agreement with the direction of the trade. Notice that the auto trend lines were pointing the way as well. The return potential here is up to 379 pips per lot.

As an additional observation, notice that the ROI appears to be squeezing together as if ready to turn up. This implies that the trader should consider exiting the bear trade and prepare for a new bull entry if additional confirmations are present to justify the entry.

FIGURE B.5 GBPUSD ST: This two-hour chart has four STs present that either were in agreement for the entry with the next opening candle, or eventually became in agreement, allowing for an entry. Remember, waiting is a good thing—if it means you are reducing risk. Waiting for the ROI to be in agreement with the trade direction is worth it. As a review from earlier entry comments, when an ST appears, the market entry will be in the opposite direction and must have an ROI in agreement. The larger the time compression, the greater the odds of success. Notice on the illustration that the last ST ran approximately 152 pips.

FIGURE B.6 EURJPY ST: This 60-minute chart illustrates an example of how the three-trade entry approach is most effective. The ST is identified. The ROI has crossed up and is in agreement with the direction of the trade. We also have a proprietary indicator telling us that buys are preferred over sells. The entry of the ST trade is the open of the candle to the right of the ST candle, which is point A. Some traders will enter three separate trades at the same time. Point B indicates the close of trade 1. Some traders will close the trade with only 20 or so pips of profit.

Point C represents the close of trade 2 because of signs of a reversal. Trade 3 is still open, but the stop is moved up to lock in 1 pip of profit. Some traders wait to see if a River X forms before closing out trade 3. By not having a limit set on trade 3, this allows the trader to take advantage of large runs in the market and over 1,000 pips.

The challenge in entering a long-term trade in order to take 1,000 pips from the market is that it requires a lot of patience and confidence in the direction of the trade. As mentioned earlier in the book, one of the issues a trader must recognize and control is that it is very easy to stay in a bad trade but very hard to stay in a good trade.

FIGURE B.7 EURJPY ST: This 60-minute chart shows a perfect ST where the ROI becomes in agreement almost immediately and the market then moves upward approximately 200 pips. The ROI is beginning to curl downward, which is a sign to consider either tightening the stop to capture as much profit as possible or just exiting the trade.

FIGURE B.8 USDJPY ST: This 30-minute chart illustrates a perfect ST with ROI agreement. The entry is the next candle open after the ST. When STs occur, there are usually many other confirmations to justify the entry.

This illustration demonstrates a market move of 121 pips. One would assume that a trader could surely obtain profits from a move as illustrated.

Although the illustration is clear regarding the 121-pip ST potential that is marked, look at the unmarked ST that occurred previous to the marked illustration. Notice that the move was delayed until the ROI began to move up after it was crossed.

FIGURE B.9 GBPJPY ST: This two-hour chart offers another example of how the three-trade entry approach is most effective. The ST is identified. The ROI has crossed down and is in agreement with the direction of the trade. We also have a proprietary indicator located at the top of the chart telling us that sells are preferred over buys.

The entry of the ST trade is the open of the candle to the right of the ST candle. Some traders will enter three separate trades at the same time. Point A represents the close of trade 1. Traders will close the trade with only 20 or so pips of profit. To the immediate right of the entry candle is a River X. This tells us that it is a good idea to remain in the trade for additional potential profits.

Point B indicates the first sign of a reversal on smaller compressions. This is due to a pullback that is forming a possible ST for the up market. Trade 2 is closed. Regarding the trade 2 exit, the ROI continues to bear down, which would normally mean that trade 2 was exited prematurely; however, the objective of the trade 2 entry is to exit the trade at the first sign of trouble.

Trade 3 is still open, but the stop is moved up to lock in 1 pip of profit or 0 (even), and as the reader can see, the combo never comes back to the original entry point. Instead, the third entry moves down considerably to point C. Point C shows where trade 3 could be closed. Another option at point C is to lock in more profits. A larger compression than this two-hour chart might tell us if more profits are possible. By not setting a limit on trade 3, the trader can take advantage of large runs in the market.

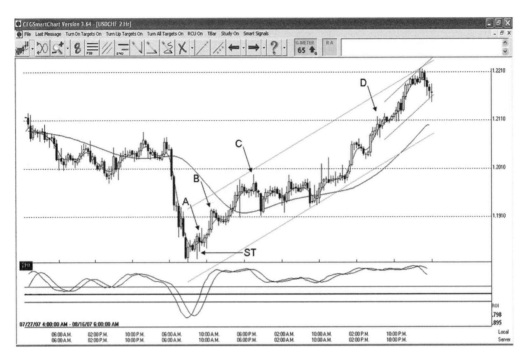

FIGURE B.10 USDCHF ST: Here is another example of how the three-trade entry approach is most effective. The ST is identified. The ROI has crossed up and is in agreement with the direction of the trade. The ROI was not strong enough as a stand-alone reason to enter the market. The delayed ST that appeared after the ROI crossed up provides us with a confirmation to enter the trade. The two-hour SmartChart also has a proprietary indicator found at the top of the chart called the G-meter, which indicates possible direction of market; it also is in agreement with the ST and ROI direction, and all of these are confirmations to trade up.

Point A represents the entry points. Here we are viewing a three-entry trade plan. Trade 1 has a 20-pip limit. Point B indicates where the 20 pips of profit were achieved. Point C indicates where trade 2 is closed on the first signs of a reversal.

Trade 2 provided over 45 pips of profit.

Trade 3 is still open, but the stop is moved up to lock in 1 pip of profit. Point D indicates where the temporary reversal ends. By not having a limit set on trade 3, the trader is able to take advantage of large runs in the market. When the combo finally reaches the upper trend wall for a strike, notice that the market bounces off of the trend wall and causes the ROI to begin widening downward, indicating where either trade 3 should be closed or the stop should be tightened to maximize profits.

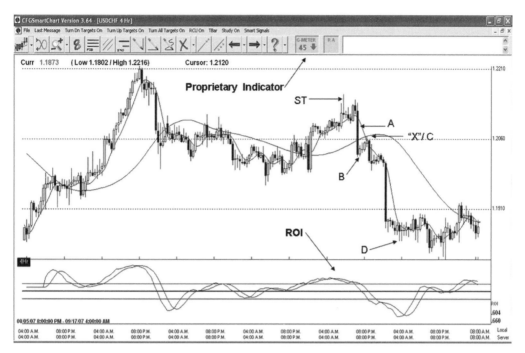

FIGURE B.11 USDCHF ST: Here is another example of how the three-trade entry approach is most effective. In this four-hour chart the ST is identified. The ROI has crossed down and is in agreement with the direction of the trade. We also have a proprietary indicator telling us that sells are preferred over buys.

Point A is the close of trade 1 with only 20 pips of profit. Trade 1 had a 20-pip limit under the rules of this three-entry strategy.

Point B indicates a possible reversal in the market. Trade 2 is closed at the first sign of a reversal, with over 40 pips of profit.

Point C indicates a River X where some traders may stay with their third trade. Trade 3 is still open, but the stop is moved up to lock in 1 pip of profit. By not having a limit set on trade 3, the trader can take advantage of large runs in the market. Point D indicates where trade 3 was closed because the ROI gave a bull X cross, which implies a possible reversal. An alternative close is to tighten the stop and allow the market to exit the trade naturally. The only benefit to this natural type of close is that the market may not exit the trade and could continue on with its bearish move, allowing even greater profits.

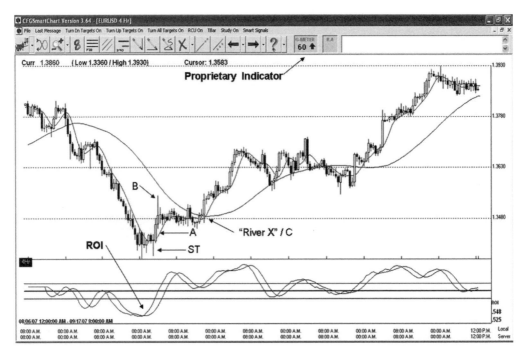

FIGURE B.12 EURUSD ST: Here is another example of how the three-trade entry approach is most effective. In this four-hour chart the ST is identified. The ROI has crossed up and is in agreement with the direction of the trade. (Note: It does not matter which signal comes first; what is important is that both are in agreement. Only then can a trader look for additional reasons to enter before making the final decision to risk money in the markets.) We also have a proprietary indicator telling us that buys are preferred over sells. The entry of the ST trade is the open of the candle to the right of the ST candle. Using the three-trade entry strategy, a trader may consider entering three separate trades at the same time—at the open of the first candle after the ST. (Larger compressions with an ST have been found to have better odds of a successful or profitable trade entry.)

Point A represents the close of trade 1. Some traders will close the trade with only 20 or so pips of profit. Point B indicates the first signs of a reversal on smaller compressions, and trade 2 is closed. Point C is a River X—a sign for some traders to remain in the trade for additional profits that the market may offer. Trade 3 is still open, but the stop is moved up to lock in 1 pip of profit. By not having a limit set on trade 3, the trader can take advantage of large runs in the market. This chart illustrates that the market has moved over 500 pips.

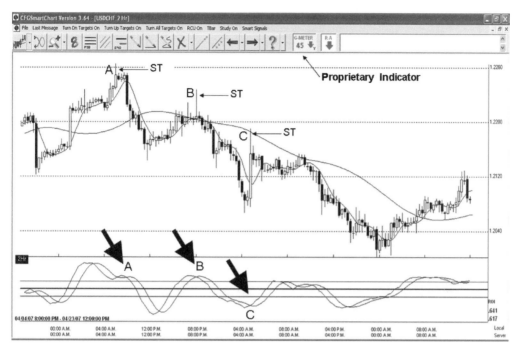

FIGURE B.13 USDCHF ST: Here is another example of the three-trade entry approach. In this two-hour chart the STs are indicated by points A, B, and C. We also have a proprietary indicator telling us that sells are preferred over buys. The position of the ROI plays a major role in deciding if a trade should be entered. Points A and B have the ROI crossed to go down—in agreement with the trade. Point C has the ROI in the wrong direction. STs A and B are the two safest trades, and an experienced selective trader would pass on ST C even though if would have paid a profit. The lack of a proper confirmation, combined with a trader's inability to tell the future, means ST C's increased risk does not justify an entry. The key is to select safe trades and pass up the not-so-safe trades.

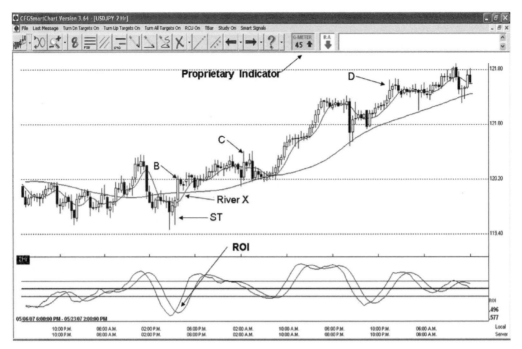

FIGURE B.14 USDJPY ST: Here is another example of the three-trade entry approach. In this two-hour chart the ST is identified. The ROI has crossed up and is in agreement with the direction of the trade. The proprietary indicator is also telling us that buys are preferred over sells. The entry of the ST trade is the open of the candle to the right of the ST candle. Some traders will enter three separate trades at the same time.

Point B indicates the close of trade 1. Some traders will close a trade with only 20 or so pips of profit.

Point C represents the close of trade 2—closed on signs of a reversal.

Trade 3 is still open, but the stop has moved up to lock in 1 pip of profit. By not having a limit set on trade 3, the trader can take advantage of large runs in the market—in this case over 200 pips.

Point D is a level to consider exiting or tightening the stop to maximize profits. If there are larger time compressions available to determine if the market is going to continue upward, traders may consider not exiting at point D. Whether to exit or remain in a trade should be based on additional confirmations taken from larger time compressions if all other confirmations have been exhausted.

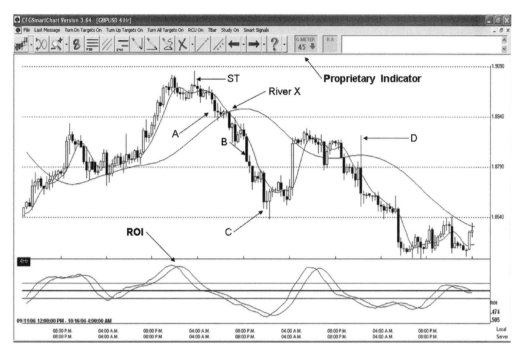

FIGURE B.15 GBPUSD ST: This example is interesting in that after the trade has started, additional ST entry opportunities begin appearing. The three-trade entry approach becomes very effective when recurring ST entry opportunities appear.

In this four-hour chart the ST is identified. The ROI has crossed down in agreement with the direction of the trade. Also, the proprietary indicator is telling us that sells are preferred over buys. The entry of the ST trade is the open of the candle to the right of the ST candle. Some traders will enter three separate trades at the same time.

Point A indicates the close of trade 1. Most traders will close the trade with only 20 or so pips of profit. Shortly after point A, a River X is formed. Some traders take advantage of a river X and stay in the trade longer, anticipating more profit.

Point B represents the close of trade 2.

Trade 3 is still open, but the stop has moved up to lock in 1 pip of profit. Point C represents the beginning of a reversal in the market. After the reversal is over a new River X is formed. After the new River X a second ST is also formed at point D. By not having a limit set on trade 3, the trader can take advantage of large runs in the market—in this case over 500 pips.

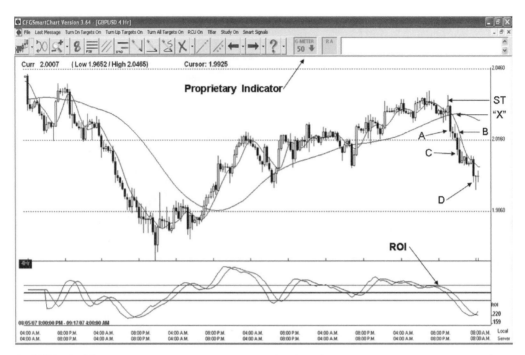

FIGURE B.16 GBPUSD ST: Here is another example of the three-trade entry approach. In this four-hour chart the ST is identified. The ROI has crossed down and is in agreement with the direction of the trade. Also, the proprietary indicator is telling us that sells are preferred over buys. The entry of the ST trade is the open of the tall black candle to the right of the ST candle.

Point A represents the close of trade 1. Even though the tall black candle is over 100 pips, many traders will close the trade with only 20 or so pips of profit. To the immediate right of the tall black candle is a River X. This is sign to remain in the trade for additional profits that may be provided.

Point B indicates where another entry is possible because of the River X.

Point C indicates where trade 2 is closed on the first signs of a reversal on smaller compressions. Trade 2 provided over 150 pips of profit.

Trade 3 is still open, but the stop is moved up to lock in 1 pip of profit. Point D shows where trade 3 is closed. The ROI has crossed up at this time. By not having a limit set on trade 3, the trader can take advantage of large runs in the market.

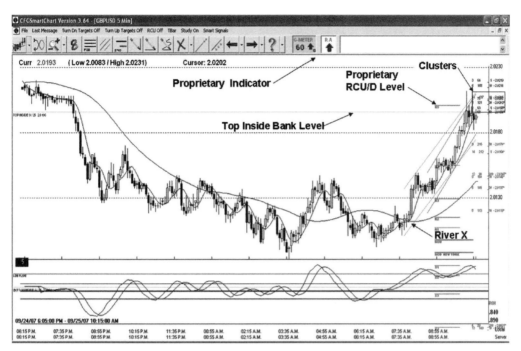

FIGURE B.17 In every trade, the more confirmations present before entering the trade, the better. For example, within the GBPUSD five-minute chart the first confirmation is the proprietary indicator, which has an up arrow, indicating buys are more favorable than sells. Next, take a look at what SmartCharts refers to as the bank level. The first bank level illustrated on the chart is identified as a top inside, level, which is the top side of a inner channel within a given historical range.

Next, look at another SmartChart proprietary indicator: the RCU/D level. In this example the R5 level is right above the top inside bank level, adding strength to this level for the market. Another proprietary indicator to consider is the target. When there are multiple targets in the same area, we refer to them as a cluster. Clusters in the market are often made up of fresh targets or are conglomerated with other valuable historical levels. In this example the clusters are inside a box that was added to the picture for demonstration purposes only. The bottom of the clusters box sits exactly on the top inside bank level. This is just one more confirmation that solidifies this as a strong area for the market to reach.

As an additional observation for a future bear trade, when the market finally reaches the bull target as illustrated and the ROI crosses down on a larger compression, it is time to look for other bear confirmations to appear. The five-minute ROI curl that is illustrated is not enough to justify an entry unless several other time compressions are in agreement with the possible bear entry.

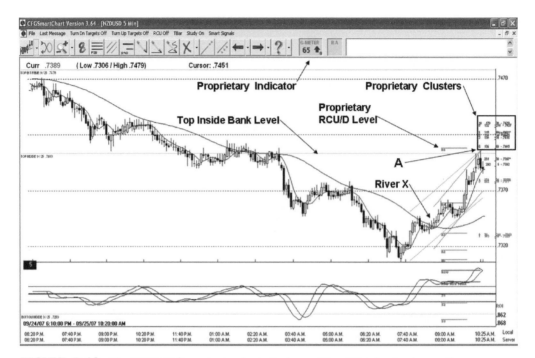

FIGURE B.18   The NZDUSD five-minute chart displays a River X trade. As always, the more confirmations, the better the trade. The first confirmation is the proprietary indicator, which has an up arrow indicating buys are more favorable than sells. This market directional arrow is found at the top of the SmartChart. The first indicator to consider is the first bank level. In this example this is a top inside bank level.

Another proprietary indicator is the RCU/D level. In this example the R5 level is just above the top inside bank level, adding strength to this level for the market to reach.

Finally, we can consider the SmartCharts targets. When there are multiple targets in the same area we refer to them as a cluster within the market. In this example the clusters are found inside a box that was added to the picture for demonstration purposes. The bottom of the clusters box sits exactly on the R5 level. This is just one more confirmation that solidifies this as a likely level for the market to reach. Point A shows that the market reached the R5, the bottom of the clusters box, and the top inside bank level. This River X trade provided over 50 pips of profit. The best trades have more than one confirmation.

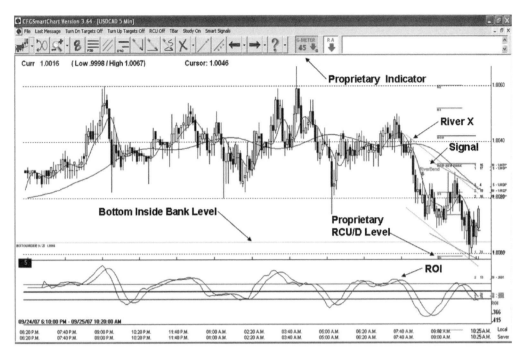

FIGURE B.19   The USDCAD five-minute chart displays a bear entry as a River X trade. As stated in other cluster illustrations, the more confirmations, the better the trade. The first confirmation is the proprietary indicator, which has a down arrow indicating sells are more favorable than buys. The first area of interest that the market may move toward is the first bank level. In this example this is the bottom inside bank level.

The next indicator to consider is the RCU/D level. In this example the S3 level is right below the bottom inside bank level, adding strength to the potential for the market to reach this level.

The ROI had just crossed down at the time of the River X, supplying one more confirmation for the sell.

Because the proprietary indicators are all pointed down, the S3 level is very close to the bottom inside wall, and the ROI crossed down at the time of the trade, a trader can enter into this position with confidence. This River X trade provided the trader with 40 pips of profit.

Glossary

appreciation   A currency is said to appreciate when it strengthens in price in response to market demand.

arbitrage   The purchase or sale of an instrument and simultaneous taking of an equal and opposite position in a related market, in order to take advantage of small price differentials between markets.

ask rate   The rate at which a financial instrument is offered for sale (as in a bid/ask spread or the sell side of the broker spread).

back office   The departments and processes related to the settlement of financial transactions.

balance of trade   The value of a country's exports minus its imports.

base currency   In general terms, the currency in which an investor or issuer maintains its book of accounts. In the forex markets, the U.S. dollar is normally considered the base currency for quotes, meaning that quotes are expressed as a unit of $1 USD per the other currency quoted in the pair. The primary exceptions to this rule are the British pound, the euro, and the Australian dollar.

bear market   A market distinguished by declining prices.

bid/ask spread   The difference between the bid and offer price, and the most widely used measure of market liquidity. Also, the spread is a fee for the broker to provide the transaction services for traders.

bid rate   The rate at which a trader is willing to buy a currency (the buy side of a broker spread).

big figure   Dealer expression referring to the first few digits of an exchange rate. These digits rarely change in normal market fluctuations, and therefore are omitted in dealer quotes, especially in times of high market activity. For example, a USD/JPY rate might be 107.30/107.35, but would be quoted verbally without the first three digits (i.e., "30/35").

book   In a professional trading environment, the summary of a trader's or desk's total positions.

broker   An individual or firm that acts as an intermediary, putting together buyers and sellers for a fee or commission. In contrast, a dealer commits capital and takes one side of a position, hoping to earn a spread (profit) by closing out the position in a subsequent trade with another party.

bull market   A market distinguished by rising prices.

Bundesbank   Germany's central bank.

cable   Trader jargon referring to the British pound/U.S. dollar exchange rate. So called because the rate was originally transmitted via a transatlantic cable beginning in the mid-1800s.

candlestick chart   A chart that indicates the trading range for a time period, as well as the opening and closing prices. If the opening price is higher than the closing price, the rectangle between the opening price and the closing price is shaded. If the closing price is higher than the opening price, that area of the chart is not shaded.

central bank   A government or quasi-governmental organization that manages a country's monetary policy. For example, the U.S. central bank is the Federal Reserve, and the German central bank is the Bundesbank.

chartist   An individual who uses charts and graphs and interprets historical data to find trends and predict future movements. Also referred to as a technical trader.

clearing   The process of settling a trade.

commission   A transaction fee charged by a broker.

confirmation   A document exchanged by counterparts to a transaction that states the terms of said transaction.

consolidation   A market that is moving sideways with a small amount of volume.

contagion   The tendency of an economic crisis to spread from one market to another. In 1997, political instability in Indonesia caused high volatility in its domestic currency, the rupiah. From there, the contagion spread to other Asian emerging currencies and then to Latin America, and is now referred to as the "Asian contagion."

contract   The standard unit of trading.

counterparty   One of the participants in a financial transaction.

country risk   Risk associated with a cross-border transaction, including, but not limited to, legal and political conditions.

cross rate   The exchange rate between any two currencies that are considered nonstandard in the country where the currency pair is quoted. For example, in the United States, a GBP/JPY quote would be considered a cross rate, whereas in the United Kingdom or Japan it would be one of the primary currency pairs traded.

currency   Any form of money issued by a government or central bank and used as legal tender and a basis for trade.

currency risk   The probability of an adverse change in exchange rates.

day trading   Refers to positions that are opened and closed on the same trading day.

dealer   An individual who acts as a principal or counterparty to a transaction. Principals take one side of a position, hoping to earn a spread (profit) by closing out the position in a subsequent trade with another party. In contrast, a broker is an individual or firm that acts as an intermediary, putting together buyers and sellers for a fee or commission.

deficit   A negative balance of trade or payments.

delivery   A forex trade where both sides make and take actual delivery of the currencies traded.

depreciation   A fall in the value of a currency due to market forces.

derivative   A contract that changes in value in relation to the price movements of a related or underlying security, future, or other physical instrument. An option is the most common derivative instrument.

devaluation   The deliberate downward adjustment of a currency's price, normally by official announcement.

downtick   A new price quote at a price lower than the preceding quote.

economic indicator   A government-issued statistic that indicates current economic growth and stability. Common indicators include employment rates, gross domestic product (GDP), inflation, retail sales, and so on.

end of day (EOD) order   An order to buy or sell at a specified price. This order remains open until the end of the trading day, which is typically 5 PM ET during the week and 4 PM ET on Fridays.

euro   The currency of the European Economic and Monetary Union (EMU). A replacement for the European Currency Unit (ECU).

European Central Bank (ECB)   The central bank for the European Economic and Monetary Union.

European Economic and Monetary Union (EMU)   The principal goal of the EMU is to establish a single European currency called the euro, which officially replaced the national currencies of the member EU countries in 2002. The current members of the EMU are Germany, France, Belgium, Luxembourg, Austria, Finland, Ireland, the Netherlands, Italy, Spain, Greece, and Portugal as well as small European states like Andorra, Monaco, San Marino, and Vatican City.

Federal Deposit Insurance Corporation (FDIC)   The regulatory agency responsible for administering bank depository insurance in the United States.

Federal Reserve (Fed)   The central bank for the United States.

Fib   Slang for Fibonacci. A Fib level is a percentage level of a measured range.

flat/square   Dealer jargon used to describe a position that has been completely reversed; for example, you bought $500,000, then sold $500,000, thereby creating a neutral (flat) position.

foreign exchange (forex, FX)   The simultaneous buying of one currency and selling of another.

forward   The prespecified exchange rate for a foreign exchange contract settling at some agreed future date, based on the interest rate differential between the two currencies involved.

forward points   The pips added to or subtracted from the current exchange rate to calculate a forward price.

fundamental analysis   Analysis of economic and political information with the objective of determining future movements in a financial market.

futures contract   An obligation to exchange a good or instrument at a set price on a future date. The primary difference between a future and a forward is that futures are typically traded over an exchange as exchange-traded contracts (ETCs), versus forwards, which are considered over-the-counter (OTC) contracts. An OTC contract is any contract *not* traded on an exchange.

good till canceled (GTC) order   An order to buy or sell at a specified price. This order remains open until filled or until the client cancels.

g-meter   A market direction meter found only on certain proprietary type charts.

hedge   A position or combination of positions that reduces the risk of your primary position.

inflation   An economic condition whereby prices for consumer goods rise, eroding purchasing power.

initial margin   The initial deposit of collateral required to enter into a position as a guarantee on future performance.

interbank rates   The foreign exchange rates at which large international banks quote other large international banks.

invasion   A term used by so-called river traders to identify the market going against the overall trend (reversal).

kiwi   Slang for New Zealand currency.

lamb market   A sideways movement of the market within a small trading range. The same as a consolidation or slow market.

leading indicator   A statistic that is considered to predict future economic activity.

limit order   An order with restrictions on the maximum price to be paid or the minimum price to be received. As an example, if the current price of USD/JPY is 102.00/05, then a limit order to buy USD would be at a price below 102.00 (e.g., 101.50).

liquidation   The closing of an existing position through the execution of an offsetting transaction.

liquidity   The ability of a market to accept large transactions with minimal to no impact on price stability.

London Interbank Offered Rate (LIBOR)   The rate used by banks when borrowing from another bank.

long position   A position that appreciates in value if market prices increase.

margin   The required equity that an investor must deposit to collateralize a position.

margin call   A request from a broker or dealer for additional funds or other collateral to guarantee performance on a position that has moved against the customer.

market maker   A dealer who regularly quotes both bid and ask prices and is ready to make a two-sided market for any financial instrument.

market risk   Exposure to changes in market prices.

mark-to-market   Process of revaluating all open positions with the current market prices. These new values then determine margin requirements.

maturity   The date for settlement or expiry of a financial instrument.

offer   The rate at which a dealer is willing to sell a currency.

offsetting transaction   A trade that serves to cancel or offset some or all of the market risk of an open position.

one cancels the other (OCO) order   A designation for two orders whereby when one of the two orders is executed the other is automatically canceled.

open order   An order that will be executed when a market moves to its designated price. Normally associated with good till canceled (GTC) orders.

open position   A deal not yet reversed or settled with a physical payment.

overnight   A trade that remains open until the next business day.

over-the-counter (OTC)   Used to describe any transaction that is not conducted over an exchange.

PCI   Percentage change indicator.

pips   Digits added to or subtracted from the fourth decimal place (i.e., 0.0001). Also called points.

political risk   Exposure to changes in governmental policy that can have an adverse effect on an investor's position.

position   The netted total holdings of a given currency.

premium   In the currency markets, describes the amount by which the forward or futures price exceeds the spot price.

price transparency   Describes quotes to which every market participant has equal access.

quote   An indicative market price, normally used for information purposes only.

rate   The price of one currency in terms of another, typically used for dealing purposes.

RCU/RCD   An acronym for River Channel Up/River Channel Down. A copyrighted and proprietary software program for CFG signature trades that determines channels in the market.

resistance   A term used in technical analysis indicating a specific price level at which analysis concludes people will sell.

revaluation   An increase in the exchange rate for a currency as a result of central bank intervention. Opposite of devaluation.

risk   Exposure to uncertain change, most often used with a negative connotation of adverse change.

risk management   The employment of financial analysis and trading techniques to reduce and/or control exposure to various types of risk.

river channel (RC)   The area enclosed by the red (fast) line and blue (slow) line on a chart.

River Oscillator Indicator (ROI)   A proprietary momentum device used for measuring historical data and calibrated closely to historical Fibonacci ratios that are derived from mathematical equations for the purpose of predicting market moves, either up or down.

river trader   One who trades in the direction of an established river using channel indicators that are in agreement with the overall trend. This group of forex traders follows the rules of trend trading, trusting signals, ignoring fundamentals, and always trading with protection.

rollover   Process whereby the settlement of a deal is rolled forward to another value date. The cost of this process is based on the interest rate differential of the two currencies.

settlement   The process by which a trade is entered into the books and records of the counterparties to a transaction. The settlement of currency trades may or may not involve the actual physical exchange of one currency for another.

short position   An investment position that benefits from a decline in market price.

sideways trading day   A trading session in which the market opens and closes at approximately the same price and may move only 20 to 80 pips.

S90/Crossover   A system that predicts targets for profit and market invasions or reversals after a target strike.

sore thumb (ST)   Nickname for a candlewick that extends far beyond the surrounding candles on a chart. It is identified usually during a moment of high volume followed by a pullback by the opposing bear or bull market, so that at the end of the compression time a very obvious candlewick is all that remains. Nicknamed by a mentor in Switzerland who was an instructor of the author.

speculator   A trader who buys or sells expecting to make a profit from market fluctuations.

spot price   The current market price. Settlement of spot transactions usually occurs within two business days.

spread   The difference between the bid and offer prices.

sterling   Refers to the British pound.

Stochastic model   A tool for estimating potential outcomes in one or more inputs over time. As applied here, a model based on the belief that as prices increase or decrease, closing prices tend to accumulate ever more closely to the highs or lows for a given period of time.

stop-loss order   Order type whereby an open position is automatically liquidated at a specific price. Often used to minimize exposure to losses if the market moves against an investor's position.

As an example, an investor who is long USD at 156.27 might wish to put in a stop-loss order at 156.01, which would limit losses should the dollar depreciate below 156.01.

support A term used in technical analysis that indicates a specific price floor at which a given exchange rate will typically correct itself. Opposite of resistance.

swap A currency swap is the simultaneous sale and purchase of the same amount of a given currency at a forward exchange rate.

technical analysis An effort to forecast prices by analyzing market data (i.e., historical price trends and averages, volumes, open interest, etc.).

tomorrow next (tom/next) Simultaneous buying and selling of a currency for delivery the following day.

transaction cost The cost of buying or selling a financial instrument.

transaction date The date on which a trade occurs.

trending day A trading session in which the market moves 80 to 300 pips upward or downward.

turnover The total money value of all executed transactions in a given time period; volume.

two-way price When both a bid and an offer rate are quoted for a forex transaction.

uptick A new price quote at a price higher than the preceding quote.

uptick rule In the United States, a regulation whereby a security may not be sold short unless the last trade prior to the short sale was at a price lower than the price at which the short sale is executed.

U.S. prime rate The interest rate at which U.S. banks will lend to their prime corporate customers.

value date The date on which counterparties to a financial transaction agree to settle their respective obligations (i.e., exchange payments). For spot currency transactions, the value date is normally two business days forward. Also known as maturity date.

volatility (vol) A statistical measure of a market's price movements over time.

whipsaw A condition of a highly volatile market where a sharp price movement is quickly followed by a sharp reversal.

world's money A term coined in 1998 by the author and used by professional traders denoting a stop order that has been moved into a profit area, in which case, should the market suddenly reverse, the personal margin is not at risk and profit is locked in place to avoid a loss.

WW A quick communication for traders in chat rooms, meaning wait and watch.

yard Slang for a billion.

Resources

Note: At the time of this writing, all sites are under revision.

Independent Forex Traders Association, LLC, www.IFxTA.org
Concorde Forex Group, Inc., www.CFGTrading.com
Concorde Group Foundation, LLC, www.ConcordeGroupFoundation.org
Forex Producers, LLC, www.Forexproducers.com

Index

Advice, last-minute, 99
Alerts, working with:
    bird-dog system, 103–104
    trading inside walls of S90/Crossover, 86,
      88, 89, 91, 92
Area, definition of, 20
Attitude, xi
Author:
    e-mail address of, 67, 106
    training and mentoring of, 9–10
Automated trend-tracking software, 82–83

Bird-dog spotting system, 103–104
Bounce trade opportunity, 61, 62, 63
Breaching extreme level, 94
Brokers:
    data feeds and, 80
    integrity of, x–xi
Bull bounce, illustration of, 88
Bullish market, marking support levels in,
    18
Buy signal, 89, 91, 92

Candlestick charts:
    Japanese, 11
    time compressions and, 79
    weekly, 59
Certified forex mentor, 2–3, 7, 8
CFG, *see* Concorde Forex Group, Inc.
Charting service, xii, 79–80
Charts, marked-up, xii
Chat room traps, 104
Cherry-type trade, 102–103
Concorde Forex Group, Inc.:
    SmartCharts and, xii, 46
    software of, 31

    trading histories and, 65
    training seminars of, x
Confirming trade entries, 103
Cost averaging:
    based on directional market trends, 56
    based on mathematical or Fibonacci levels,
      56–57
    summary of, 57
Currency combo, focusing on, 99

Daily trading tips, 102–103
Daily volume, 7
Data feed for tracking market, 80
Demo money, trading, x, 66
Development program, 6
DGB Technologies, LLC, 45–46
Disclaimers, xii
"Dogfight" section of daily market, 77
Downtrend:
    resistances in, 12–13
    working with, 60–63
Downtrend crossovers, 30
Drawing trend lines, 61

Easing-into-experience procedure, 95
Entering trade with confirmation, 96–97
Exiting early, 56–57
Extreme levels (ELs):
    five-minute charts showing, 46, 47
    as floating, 78
    knowledge and training to work with, 50,
      52
    obtaining, 79
    skills needed to trade, 79–83
    strong S90/Crossover, chart showing, 48–49
    time compressions and, 45–49, 77

139